T0334105

"There is an extended literature on qualitative methods, with much attention given to details and technicalities. But why is there a need for such approaches at all, whether they are called non-reductionist, holistic, or meaning-centered? Why do we need methods that are radically different from those used in traditional psychology? This book offers some fundamental answers to these questions. It takes a look at psychology as a whole: as the project of a comprehensive exploration of the human being in the world. And it reminds us of its still unfulfilled promises."

– Jens Brockmeier, The American University of Paris, France

"This compendium of work by distinguished scholars updates our view of psychological science to include the growing recognition of qualitative inquiry. These writers tackle the hard methodological questions and argue wisely for pluralism and integration as the future of psychology. It's a must-read for researchers."

– Ruthellen Josselson, Fielding Graduate University, USA

Situating Qualitative Methods in Psychological Science

Although qualitative approaches to psychological research have a long history in the discipline, they have also been, and remain, marginalized from the canon of mainstream scientific psychology. At the current moment, however, there is growing recognition of the importance of qualitative methods and a movement toward a more inclusive and eclectic stance on psychological research. This volume reflects upon the historical and contemporary place of qualitative methods in psychology and considers future possibilities for further integration of these methods in the discipline. Scholars representing a wide range of perspectives in qualitative and theoretical psychology reflect on the historical and contemporary positions of qualitative methods in psychology with an eye to the future of research and theory in the discipline. This book encourages a more critical and inclusive stance on research, recognizing both the limits and contributions that different methodological approaches can make to the project of psychological knowledge.

Brian Schiff is Professor and Chair of the Department of Psychology at the American University of Paris and Director of the George and Irina Schaeffer Center for the Study of Genocide, Human Rights and Conflict Prevention. He is the author of *A New Narrative for Psychology* (2017), editor of *Rereading Personal Narrative and Life Course* (2014), and co-editor of *Life and Narrative: The Risks and Responsibilities for Storying Experience* (2017).

Advances in Theoretical and Philosophical Psychology
Series Editor: Brent D. Slife
Brigham Young University

Brent D. Slife, Kari A. O'Grady, and Russell D. Kosits
The Hidden Worldviews of Psychology's Theory, Research, and Practice

Edwin E. Gantt and Richard N. Williams
On Hijacking Science: Exploring the Nature and Consequences of Overreach in Psychology

Brian Schiff
Situating Qualitative Methods in Psychological Science

For more information about this series, please visit: www.routledge.com/psychology/series/TPP

Situating Qualitative Methods in Psychological Science

Edited by Brian Schiff

Routledge
Taylor & Francis Group

LONDON AND NEW YORK

First published 2019 by Routledge

2 Park Square, Milton Park, Abingdon, Oxfordshire OX14 4RN
52 Vanderbilt Avenue, New York, NY 10017

Routledge is an imprint of the Taylor & Francis Group, an informa business

First issued in paperback 2019

Library of Congress Cataloging-in-Publication Data
Names: Schiff, Brian, editor.
Title: Situating qualitative methods in psychological science /
    [edited by] Brian Schiff.
Description: 1 Edition. | New York : Routledge, 2019. | Series:
    Advances in theoretical and philosophical psychology
Identifiers: LCCN 2018017026 | ISBN 9780815353423 (hardback :
    alk. paper) | ISBN 9781351136426 (ebook)
Subjects: LCSH: Psychology—Research. | Qualitative research.
Classification: LCC BF76.5 .S5198 2019 | DDC 150.72/1—dc23
LC record available at https://lccn.loc.gov/2018017026

ISBN: 978-0-8153-5342-3 (hbk)
ISBN: 978-0-367-45784-6 (pbk)

Typeset in Times New Roman
by Apex CoVantage, LLC

Contents

Contributors

Mark Freeman is Distinguished Professor of Ethics and Society in the Department of Psychology at the College of the Holy Cross in Worcester, Massachusetts, and has written extensively about narrative psychology, and qualitative psychology more generally, throughout his career.

Kenneth J. Gergen is Senior Research Professor in Psychology at Swarthmore College, and the President of the Taos Institute. He is known internationally for his contributions to social constructionist theory, technology and cultural change, and relational theory and practice. Among his major writings are *Realities and Relationship: Soundings in Social Construction, The Saturated Self: Dilemmas of Identity in Contemporary Life, An Invitation to Social Construction*, and *Relational Being: Beyond Self and Community*. Gergen has received numerous awards for his work, including honorary degrees in both the United States and Europe.

James T. Lamiell earned his PhD in 1976 from Kansas State University. He is now Professor Emeritus of Psychology at Georgetown University, where he was an active member of the teaching and research faculty for 36 years.

Steven R. Sabat is Professor Emeritus of Psychology at Georgetown University, the author of *The Experience of Alzheimer's Disease: Life through a Tangled Veil* (2001), *Alzheimer's Disease and Dementia: What Everyone Needs to Know* (2018), and co-editor of *Dementia: Mind, Meaning, and the Person* (2006).

Brian Schiff is Professor and Chair of the Department of Psychology at the American University of Paris and Director of the George and Irina Schaeffer Center for the Study of Genocide, Human Rights and Conflict Prevention. He is the author of *A New Narrative for Psychology* (2017), editor of *Rereading Personal Narrative and Life Course* (2014), and co-editor of *Life and Narrative: The Risks and Responsibilities for Storying Experience* (2017).

Kathleen L. Slaney is Associate Professor of Psychology at Simon Fraser University. She is a Fellow of the American Psychological Association, author of *Validating Psychological Constructs* (2017), and co-editor of *A Wittgensteinian Perspective on the Use of Conceptual Analysis in Psychology* (2013) and *The Wiley Handbook of Theoretical and Philosophical Psychology* (2015).

Donna Tafreshi is a PhD candidate in the Psychology Department at Simon Fraser University. She studies and teaches on the topics of research methods (quantitative, qualitative, and mixed), psychometrics, statistics for psychology, and the history and philosophy of psychology.

Frederick J. Wertz is Professor of Psychology, Fordham University. He is the co-author of *Five Ways of Doing Qualitative Analysis: Phenomenological Psychology, Grounded Theory, Discourse Analysis, Narrative Research, and Intuitive Inquiry* (2011), and past president of the Society for Qualitative Inquiry in Psychology.

Series Editor's Foreword

Psychologists need to face the facts. Their commitment to empiricism for answering disciplinary questions does not prevent pivotal questions from arising that cannot be evaluated empirically, hence the title of this series: *Advances in Theoretical and Philosophical Psychology*. Such questions as: What is the relation between mind and body? What is the nature of a good life? And even: Are current psychological methods adequate to truly understand the person? These questions are in some sense philosophical, to be sure, but the discipline of psychology cannot advance even its own empirical agenda without addressing questions like these in defensible ways. Indeed, it could be argued that there is no empirical evidence for the philosophy of empiricism itself!

How then should the discipline of psychology deal with such non-empirical questions? We could leave the answers exclusively to professional philosophers, but this would mean that the conceptual foundations of the discipline, including the conceptual framework of empiricism itself, are left to scholars who are *outside* the discipline. As undoubtedly helpful as philosophers are and would be, this situation would mean that the people doing the actual psychological work, psychologists themselves, are divorced from the people who formulate and re-formulate the conceptual foundations of that work. This division of labor would seem dangerous to the long-term viability of the discipline.

Instead, the founders of psychology—thinkers such as Wundt, Freud, and James—recognized the importance of psychologists themselves in formulating their own foundations. These parents of psychology not only did their own theorizing, in cooperation with many others; they realized the significance of constantly re-examining these theories and philosophies, including the theories and philosophies of psychology's methods. The people most involved in the discipline's activities would thus be the ones most knowledgeable about whether and how such changes needed to be made. This series is dedicated to the examining and re-examining of these foundations.

The present book is a wonderful instance of this examining, as it seeks to understand the foundations of psychology's methods. Most psychological researchers would likely admit to two broad categories of these methods, quantitative and qualitative. Yet, the roles and relations between these categories of inquiry have long eluded the discipline. Are they, for example, methodological tools of equal status, like the mallet and chisel of a sculpture's tool box? There seems to be no question that qualitative research is usually a poor step-child to quantitative research, at least in many disciplinary quarters. But is this inequality justified, and if not, what is the unique contribution of qualitative inquiry?

Perhaps even more challenging is the growing popularity of psychological research that *combines* the two tools of inquiry—mixed method inquiry. Here, especially, individual researchers have been forced on the spot to formulate the relations between these two divergent categories of methods to interpret their data. How satisfactorily have they done so? Fortunately, the present volume, *Situating Qualitative Methods in Psychological Science*, rides to the rescue in a rigorous and yet practical fashion. It addresses all these questions and so many others as it explains not only the relationship between these methods but also how they might be understood and used in a complementary manner for the future of psychological research.

Brent D. Slife

Introduction

Situating Qualitative Methods in Psychological Science

Brian Schiff

One doesn't need to dig deep to recognize that quantitative methods are intensely imbricated with disciplinary psychology. At every level, psychological *research methods* are commonly equated with *quantitative methods*. At the entryway to the discipline when training undergraduate and graduate students, the core courses on research methods are concerned almost entirely with the design and analysis of psychometric instruments (scales, surveys, and questionnaires), experiments, and statistical techniques of data analysis. The hegemony of quantitative methods is also strikingly apparent in research publications; the highest ranked journals in virtually every area of psychology exclusively publish quantitative research.

This volume is not an argument against the utility or importance of quantitative methods. In many contexts, these methods are useful and powerful tools that aid the development of our understanding of human beings. The problem is that psychology has long maintained that there is only one legitimate pathway to scientific knowledge—quantitative, reductive, and probabilistic. Danziger (1990) and Allport (cited in Bruner, 1990) referred to this uncritical devotion to quantitative methods as the single, and unquestioned, approach to scientific psychology as "methodolatry." Although quantitative methods can be useful tools, they have been stretched and over-extended beyond what they can credibly tell us about human psychology. Indeed, the exclusive use of quantitative methods seems to imply that every possible psychological question can be, and must be, answered using quantitative representations and statistical forms of analysis. However, there remain considerable, and hereto uncharted, regions of human psychology—central to the fundamental mission of the discipline and deserving of serious and sustained exploration—that cannot be adequately or fully approached using such methods. This is the discipline's disastrous contradiction: Qualitative methods are essential to research the basic problems of human psychology; however, such methods are believed unscientific and, therefore, outside the purview of psychology as a science.

Although qualitative approaches to psychological research have a long history in the discipline, they have also been, and remain, marginalized— banished from the canon of scientific psychology. However, at the current moment, there appears to be an increasing recognition of the importance of qualitative methods and a movement toward a more inclusive and eclectic stance on psychological research. Is psychology on the verge of a major revision in its conception of research methods? There are some good reasons to think so. In 2013, the journal *Qualitative Psychology*, published by the American Psychological Association (APA), was inaugurated. In 2014, Division 5 of the APA voted to change its name from "Evaluation, Measurement & Statistics" to "Quantitative and Qualitative Methods." Journals and publications employing combined qualitative and quantitative methods, so-called *mixed methods*, are on the rise and receiving increased attention as a means for more comprehensively addressing research problems. Furthermore, the American Psychological Association's Publications and Communications Board Working Group on Journal Article Reporting Standards for Qualitative Research (Levitt et al., 2018) recently published in the *American Psychologist* standards to guide authors, editors, and reviewers in the evaluation and critique of research employing qualitative methods.

This movement toward qualitative methods is significant and encouraging. However, to move productively forward, many critical problems remain for us to grapple with. Indeed, the discipline, as a whole, needs to arrive at a consensual understanding of methods in which qualitative methods are accorded legitimacy as a viable pathway to psychological knowledge. Given the long-standing antipathy to qualitative methods, this is by no means an easy task. But, I remain convinced that a radical change in the discipline's methodological orientation is not only necessary, but is also possible. Furthermore, I believe that convincing reasons and sound evidence are the best route to effectuate such a sea change; this is the spirit of this collection of essays.

This volume reflects on the historical and contemporary place of qualitative methods in psychology and future possibilities for further integration of these methods in the discipline. Scholars representing a wide range of perspectives in qualitative and theoretical psychology present their views on the place of qualitative methods in psychological science with an eye to the future shape of research in the discipline and the philosophy of science undergirding research practices. Taken as a whole, the contributions to this volume argue for opening the discipline to a more critical and inclusive stance on research methods that recognizes the limits and contributions that different methodological approaches can make to the project of psychological knowledge.

The overarching problem of this volume, situating qualitative methods in scientific psychology, raises three substantive questions: (1) What has been, is, and should be the relationship between quantitative and qualitative methods? (2) Are qualitative methods a part of psychological science, or are they something else? (3) What is the unique contribution of qualitative methods in the production of psychological knowledge?

Quantitative and Qualitative Methods

Quantitative methods are often juxtaposed against qualitative methods as if the two are in competition or at conflict with each other, engaged in a kind of methods war. The battle lines are, presumably, demarcated by radically different philosophies of science, which guide research programs toward, on the one hand, the objective tools of inquiry of the natural sciences or, on the other hand, the subjective approaches adopted in the humanities (Slaney & Tafreshi, this volume). However, the war metaphor is, at best, highly inaccurate, implying that methods are mutually exclusive and incompatible, and, at worst, corrosive, pitting researchers and research agendas against one another. There are numerous historical examples of research programs that seamlessly weave together qualitative and quantitative methods (See Wertz, this volume). Moreover, philosophy of science does not, necessarily, determine method choice (Slaney & Tafreshi, this volume). Despite our preconceptions, qualitative researchers can draw upon a positivist or post-positivist philosophy of science, while quantitative researchers can draw upon a social constructionist or hermeneutic one (See Gergen, this volume and Slaney & Tafreshi, this volume). But, if the conflict metaphor is not the right one, then, how should psychologists, in theory and in practice, characterize the relationship between quantitative and qualitative methods?

Although the Manichean cleavage of research into qualitative and quantitative archetypes might be of heuristic value, the borders are not as clear-cut as we might imagine. First and foremost, all quantitative approaches rely upon the skills of interpretation. As Wertz (this volume) argues, "Quantitative knowing is necessarily based on and is impossible without qualitative knowledge" (p. 45). It is, for Wertz, "primary." Numbers are not transparent—they don't just interpret themselves. Understanding what numbers mean requires qualitative knowledge and considerable interpretive acumen to construct a coherent argument, or story, out of the data (Sabat, this volume; Slife & Williams, 1995; Wertz, this volume). In some quantitative techniques, interpretation is even more evident and explicit. For instance, factor analytic methods apply a qualitative reading to patterns in counted data. Similarly, qualitative data are commonly coded, reduced to quantitative categories, and submitted to statistical analysis (*cf.*, Haden & Hoffman,

2013). Furthermore, as Wertz (this volume) argues, qualitative methods are integrated in numerous research programs, with no inherent contradiction. In fact, as Wertz shows, qualitative methods can be valuable alongside quantitative methods, at all stages of the research process and for multiple purposes, such as developing instruments and hypotheses for quantitative research or even interpreting quantitative analyses and analyzing anomalies.

At the heart of the emerging methodological inclusiveness is the argument that qualitative and quantitative methods can be fruitfully, and pragmatically, integrated according to the nature of the research question under investigation (Slaney & Tafreshi, this volume). No single approach or method can describe and understand the full range and complexity of human psychology. Rather, multiple strategies are required. Psychological phenomena come in all different forms, requiring researchers to make flexible choices in their methods of study. For better or for worse, there is no essential methodological formula that can be applied to all research problems.

In their call for a critical methodology, Yanchar, Gantt, and Clay (2005) argue for researchers to adapt their research programs to the unique features of the problem or question under study. Part of the argument for any particular piece of research, usually unstated, is an argument for the methods themselves—a research argument. We need to ask: How well does this particular method capture the relevant aspects of the phenomenon of interest for study? The thrust of a critical methodology is for all research, quantitative and qualitative, to raise the visibility of the research argument so that the bridge between problem and method is open for reflection and criticism, and we can start to produce more credible research arguments by more sensibly coupling research problems with methods.

Within theoretical, critical, and qualitative psychology, there is a sustained discussion of methods. Qualitative researchers often include extensive justifications for, and criticisms of, the credibility of their method to respond to their research question. The reflexive practice of methodological critique is largely missing in mainstream conversations employing quantitative methods. In my view, practicing critical reflexivity on all research arguments, both qualitative and quantitative, would be a productive strategy of managing the split between qualitative and quantitative methods that would enhance the validity and trustworthiness of all psychological research (Gough & Madill, 2012). Rather than relying on disciplinary tradition and imposing an unsuitable method, psychologists would be much better served to ask a simple question: What is the best method for studying this problem?

This volume argues that the discipline stands to benefit from a more pragmatic, and less politicized, understanding of methods. Dogmatic adherence to a single methodological approach inherently contradicts the openness and flexibility necessary for innovative scientific discovery. Rather than perpetuate the myth that qualitative and quantitative methods are mutually exclusive and incompatible, the discipline should embrace possibilities for new models of the research enterprise. In this sense, methods, quantitative and qualitative, can be viewed as value-neutral tools that, skillfully and meticulously applied, can provide evidence to help us think through particular research questions. Although, as Slaney and Tafreshi (this volume) argue, researchers should critically reflect upon their philosophical commitments, methods are not political or ideological choices, but the means for studying and describing phenomena in the most efficacious manner and for making arguments about discoveries.

Scientific Psychology

The problem of method, of course, is closely related to fundamental conceptions of what constitutes science. The term *psychological science*, in the title of this volume, is deliberately employed to provoke debate about the scientific status of qualitative methods. And, going one step further, I intended to raise the question about what fundamentally makes any method, quantitative or qualitative, scientific. Typically, psychologists consider quantitative methods as *the one and only* "scientific" psychology and place qualitative methods in some other marginal category—perhaps art, literature, journalism, or philosophy, but not psychological science. But are such blanket characterizations warranted? Are qualitative methods any less scientific than quantitative ones? Do qualitative methods fundamentally change the meaning of psychological science?

Science is uniformly included in definitions of psychology, and the notion of science is central to the identity of the discipline as a whole. But, definitions of science, in psychology and elsewhere, are notoriously elusive and conceptually problematic. Science is employed as an indexical term, without a fixed referent, variously referring to one or more aspects of the processes or procedures of research, the attitude of the researcher, or even the authority or truth-value of observations and theories. Certainly, numbers, statistics, tables, and diagrams *appear* less subjective and more scientific than the thick descriptions of words and meanings characteristic of qualitative research, but there must be more essential properties to science than style. Precisely, what is it that makes research scientific?

In psychology, we typically answer that psychology is scientific because researchers employ *the* scientific method. But, just which scientific method are we talking about? As Slife and Williams (1995) write "There is no such thing as *the* scientific method. There are as many scientific methods as there are scientists doing research" (p. 169). Despite the diverse approaches to science, they continue "there are, however, some commonalities among scientists in the sort of methods they use, so it is possible to study their methods and talk about what qualifies as science" (p. 169). But, there are limits to such a descriptive, bottom-up approach. Even in the more restricted sphere of qualitative methods, there is no single qualitative method, but multiple strategies for studying and describing psychological phenomena. As Gergen (this volume) describes, qualitative methods represent an eclectic set of approaches with diverse epistemological and ontological points of view and varied applications. The same is true about quantitative methods in psychology. Despite the merger of correlational and experimental psychology around probabilistic statistics (see Lamiell, this volume), there remains a pluralistic array of quantitative approaches to design, measurement, and analysis. Of course, one can also find methodological pluralism in the natural sciences. The methods of a biologist studying genetic inheritance or botany are so strikingly different from a physicist studying the properties of light that we would be hard pressed to say that they are both using a common scientific method. Although it seems like a trivial truism, the complexity of human psychology, from the biological to the interpretive to the cultural, demands that psychologists be even more resourceful and innovative in their pursuit of knowledge.

Qualitative researchers have a range of opinions on these matters. Some embrace the artist quality of their scholarship or view their research as outside of the narrow frame of science. In the concluding chapter, Freeman (this volume) offers a complex view that accommodates forms of qualitative research aimed at the production and accumulation of knowledge and those that are more "art-ful," both of which can contain a "deep scientificity" by producing "a dimension of meaning that transcends its own particularity" (p. 110). However, most understand their research as employing *a* scientific method and reject the characterization of their research as somehow standing outside of scientific psychology. Although each of the contributions to this volume has their own position, each views qualitative research as integral in accounting for the complexity of human experience and the development of psychological knowledge.

In the end, this volume can be understood as an appeal for a more capacious definition of psychological science, which would include qualitative methods at the very heart of the discipline. Rather than thinking about psychological science as the application of *the* scientific method, the discipline would be better served by considering science as a range of strategies, necessarily pluralistic, of critically engaging problems to arrive at trustworthy knowledge claims. As Lamiell (this volume) argues, somewhat playfully, the analysis of the etymological roots of science "in the language of the land where experimental psychology was born," *Wissenschaft*, points the way to a "broad—and historically valid—understanding of science." He writes, "In its broadest sense, therefore, 'science' can be characterized as an activity devoted to the '*schaffen*-ing' of *Wissen*, i.e., the doing or making or creating of knowledge" (p. 23). In a similar vein, Polkinghorne (1983) points out, that the etymological roots of "the word method is thus 'a going after' or 'a pursuit.' In the case of science, it is a pursuit of knowledge" (p. 4).

In this pursuit, methods should be specifically crafted to studying particular phenomena or problems and making them available for description, insight, and understanding. The deliberate choice of which method to use out of our toolkit, as Slaney and Tafreshi (this volume) argue, should be a pragmatic decision about what works best in disclosing and opening up the problem or phenomenon under consideration for meticulous analysis. As Freeman (2011) argues, "the most fundamental obligation of scientific inquiry—[is] to be faithful to the phenomena one seeks to explore" (p. 391). Freeman further adds that in order to become more faithful, "paradoxically . . . *psychology can reach a greater, more authentic mode of scientificity precisely by becoming more art-ful in at least a portion of what it does*" (p. 390). In other words, inverting the paradigm that the more psychology imitates the hard sciences the more it becomes scientific, the pathway to a fruitful scientific psychology might entail the inclusion of methods, deceptively artistic or literary in their style, which are better suited to describing certain basic aspects of human psychology. In such a way, qualitative methods become essential to the project of psychological science, providing the means to research fundamental psychological phenomena that are inaccessible to quantification.

Qualitative Insights

In a sense, there is nothing revolutionary about the argument for the inclusion of alternative approaches beyond statistical and experimental methods to understand the breadth and context of human experience. Even Wundt understood the need for complimentary, non-experimental methods, to understand the higher psychological processes, arguing for the necessity of communication and collaboration between experimental and descriptive methods (Cole, 1996; Lamiell, this volume). As Lamiell (this volume) points out, Stern recognized long ago the need for multiple research strategies in the study of individuality. Furthermore, it is a long-standing contention of philosophical hermeneutics that the study of human experience requires the development of interpretive methods that are uniquely suited to the phenomenon (Gadamer, 1960/1993; Ricoeur, 1981; Taylor, 1971). Over a hundred years ago, Dilthey (1894/1976) called for establishing the human sciences, based upon empathic understanding and the principles of interpretation theory, alongside the natural science approach to psychological knowledge. But, the dream of integrating interpretive methods into the center of the discipline, unfortunately, has never been fulfilled.

There are many sound reasons for valorizing qualitative methods. Clearly, some psychological phenomena are difficult or even impossible to quantify. Indeed, when we start to explore the realm of human experience and meaning making, quantitative methods are clumsy and, oftentimes, misleading tools. But, the hegemony of quantitative methods impels researchers to study every possible psychological problem, reductively and statistically, as a variable-centered problem. No justifications are required; it is just assumed that all psychological phenomena can be studied with quantitative tools.

This is a dangerous assumption, which leads to numerous errors in our understanding of the dynamics of human psychology. As Lamiell (2003, this volume) has argued, psychologists perpetuate a long-standing, and fatal, logical error when using group-level statistical analyses to deduce what is thought to be happening, at least to some extent, at the level of person. However, statistical relationships between persons do not translate to the phenomenal experience of persons. This fundamental and implicit inference, ubiquitous in the interpretation of quantitative research, is completely erroneous and damaging to the integrity of our research. But, we continue to interpret these statistical relationships *as if* they describe how persons think. Lamiell (2003) names this logical error the "Thorndike maneuver."

In a sense, qualitative methods allow researchers to access and observe psychological phenomena in a manner that is inaccessible to quantitative research. There are many facets to this argument, but I would like to highlight two critical insights, not observable through quantitative means, that qualitative methods add to our understanding of human psychology. First, qualitative research enables explorations that go beyond and beneath the superficial fact that two variables are correlated in the group to describe the dynamic connections that persons make in their own reflections and interpretations. As Sabat (this volume) argues, qualitative methods uncover sense-making practices in action—in the experiencing person. In such a way, qualitative methods open up for analysis the subjective world of persons, making experience and the basic psychological processes of interpretation and meaning making apparent and observable. By making visible the ways that persons construct and connect their experiences, how they reason and think through self and world, qualitative methods are a corrective force to Lamiell's (2003) Thorndike maneuver. Second, qualitative methods provide researchers with insight into the context of psychological phenomena. Psychological phenomena are not static variables, but are part of the thoughts and lives of real persons, who are engaged in social relationships and embedded in history and culture. As I argue (Schiff, this volume) qualitative methods provide the tools for understanding basic psychological processes in context, across levels of analysis, as part of the person, but also part of the social world. Qualitative research provides the language for more dense and complex descriptions of *how*, *where*, and *when* persons think, feel, and act to develop synthetic theories about *why*.

The discipline could draw a sharp line and say that psychology is not concerned with how persons, alone and together, make sense of themselves and the world and relegate these core psychological problems to other disciplines. However, this would be a strange stance for a science of thought and action. Better, it could enlarge the scope of inquiry and welcome innovative methods for studying and theorizing about psychology into the center of the conversation.

It is high time that we resolve this internecine debate on the status of qualitative methods in psychology. Although I am optimistic about the various developments in the field, which seem to point to an opening for qualitative methods, the future shape of the field doesn't depend solely on the willingness of those committed to the qualitative project, such as myself and the authors of this volume, to remain engaged. The argument for the integration of qualitative methods into mainstream psychology has been elaborated over many years (*cf.*, Allport, 1942/1951, 1962) and, unfortunately, with only limited success. Certainly, qualitative methods have become more developed and refined over the years, and the argument for inclusion of qualitative methods is now sharp and sophisticated (Lamiell, 2003, this volume; Schiff, 2017). But, the success of this emerging methodological inclusiveness relies upon the willingness of mainstream quantitative researchers to adopt these arguments or, at the very least, to engage with them. Until this moment, the mainstream has viewed qualitative methods as a threat to the integrity of scientific psychology. It most certainly is not. If anything, qualitative methods are a pathway to enhancing the scientific value of psychological knowledge. It is my view that this recognition must shape the future of psychology.

The aspiration of this volume is to engage mainstream quantitative researchers in a dialogue on the future shape of psychological research. We hope to move beyond the destructive dogmatic polarization that mythologizes this dialogue as an entrenched methods war and onto new models for collaboration on a common project—understanding the mysteries of human thought, action, and feeling. It is our contention that psychological science can move forward only when a productive, and consensual, relationship between qualitative and quantitative methods develops. This volume offers a pathway to a more comprehensive and thoughtful stance on psychological methods.

References

Allport, G. W. (1942/1951). *The use of personal documents in psychological research*. New York, NY: Social Science Research Council.

Allport, G. W. (1962). The general and the unique in psychological science. *Journal of Personality*, *30*(3), 405–422.

Bruner, J. (1990). *Acts of meaning*. Cambridge, MA: Harvard University Press.

Cole, M. (1996). *Cultural psychology: A once and future discipline*. Cambridge, MA: Harvard University Press.

Danziger, K. (1990). *Constructing the subject: Historical origins of psychological research*. New York, NY: Cambridge University Press.

Dilthey, W. (1894/1976). *Selected writings* (H. P. Rickman, Ed. & Trans.). New York, NY: Cambridge University Press.

Freeman, M. (2011). Toward poetic science. *Integrative Psychological and Behavioral Science*, *45*(4), 389–396. doi:10.1007/s12124-011-9171-x

Gadamer, H. G. (1960/1993). *Truth and method: Second* (Rev. ed., J. Weinsheimer & D. G. Marshall, Trans.). New York, NY: Continuum.

Gough, B., & Madill, A. (2012). Subjectivity in psychological science: From problem to prospect. *Psychological Methods*, *17*(3), 374–384. doi:10.1037/ a0029313

Haden, C. A., & Hoffman, P. C. (2013). Cracking the code: Using personal narratives in research. *Journal of Cognition and Development*, *14*(3), 361–375. doi:10 .1080/15248372.2013.805135

Lamiell, J. T. (2003). *Beyond individual and group differences: Human individuality, scientific psychology, and William Stern's critical personalism*. Thousand Oaks, CA: Sage Publications.

Levitt, H. M., Bamberg, M., Creswell, J. W., Frost, D. M., Josselson, R., & Suárez-Orozco, C. (2018). Journal article reporting standards for qualitative primary, qualitative meta-analytic, and mixed methods research in psychology: The APA Publications and Communications Board task force report. *American Psychologist*, *73*(1), 26–46. doi:10.1037/amp0000151

Polkinghorne, D. (1983). *Methodology for the human sciences: Systems of inquiry*. Albany, NY: State University of New York Press.

Ricoeur, P. (1981). *Hermeneutics and the human sciences* (J. B. Thompson, Ed. & Trans.). Cambridge: Cambridge University Press.

Schiff, B. (2017). *A new narrative for psychology*. New York, NY: Oxford University Press.

Slife, B. D., & Williams, R. N. (1995). *What's behind the research? Discovering hidden assumptions in the behavioral sciences*. Thousand Oaks, CA: Sage Publications.

Taylor, C. (1971). Interpretation and the sciences of man. *The Review of Metaphysics*, *25*(1), 3–51.

Yanchar, S. C., Gantt, E. E., & Clay, S. L. (2005). On the nature of a critical methodology. *Theory & Psychology*, *15*(1), 27–50. doi:10.1177/0959354305049743

1 Some Historical Perspective on the Marginalization of Qualitative Methods Within Mainstream Scientific Psychology

James T. Lamiell

The laudable conceit of the present volume is that "qualitative methods are moving from the periphery to the center of psychological research" (Schiff, this volume, Introduction). However valid this claim might be, it leaves begging the question of how qualitative methods were relegated to the periphery of psychological research to begin with. The purpose of this chapter is to highlight some of the major developments unfolding from the late nineteenth century through the first half of the twentieth century that produced this outcome. Although the subject matter of this chapter is thus primarily historical, it is my hope that the critical perspective it offers will help to soften the abiding resistance within the mainstream to the full-fledged incorporation of qualitative methods into the discipline's research methods canon.

On the "Quantitative Imperative" in Psychology

Without question, a phenomenon on which the Australian scholar Joel Michell has written extensively, namely, the phenomenon of the "quantitative imperative" in the methodological canon of mainstream psychology, has been a major force in the discipline's historical marginalization of qualitative methods (see, e.g., Michell, 2003, 2004, 2011, 2016). Put succinctly, the quantitative imperative is the idea that *measurement* is a necessary feature of science. This conviction gained the upper hand among mainstream experimental psychologists virtually from the time of its mythical birth in Wilhelm Wundt's (1832–1920) Leipzig laboratory in 1879, and although the assumptions of that conviction have been challenged by countless authors over the decades, it continues to dominate (see Gergen, this volume). As Michell (2004) himself put matters: "[The quantitative] imperative is deeply ingrained in psychology and most psychologists believe that if you are going to study something scientifically then you have to measure it" (p. 310).

Of course, in order for it to be sensible to attempt to measure some psychological attribute or variable, one must assume, at least provisionally, that the attribute or variable is measurable. To the early experimentalists this meant, following the apparent lead of physics, that the variable should be expressible quantitatively on a scale by means of which discrete amounts of that variable could not only be properly ordered relative to, but also meaningfully added to or subtracted from, one another. These properties, Michell has noted, were not properties to be assumed a priori by the investigator but, rather, were properties to be established empirically, as, for example, in classical Fechnerian psychophysics. The failure to do so could be seen as evidence against the provisional assumption that the attribute or variable was genuinely *measurable* to begin with.

Outside the domain of psychophysics, however, the criteria for genuine measurement in the classically understood sense came to be seen within psychology more as aspirational standards than as preconditions for proceeding quantitatively. As the psychological testing movement proliferated, beginning early in the twentieth century, the performances of research subjects were being represented numerically and analyzed computationally in ways that *assumed*, minimally, the property of additivity adhering to interval scales of measurement, absent any independent evidence that the scales in use actually had interval and not merely ordinal scale properties. Implicitly underway here was an understanding of "measurement" that S. S. Stevens (1906–1973) would eventually characterize explicitly as "a set of conventions governing the assignment of numerals to objects or events according to rules" (Stevens, 1946, p. 677).

Unlike the original, classical conception of measurement modeled on physics, this conception of measurement embraced by psychologists does not raise the question: Is "it" (whatever "it" might be) measurable? On the contrary, this view allows that, in principle, *anything* is measurable, because there are, in principle, no limits to the conventions that can be established for assigning numerals to the objects or events of interest. This revised understanding of measurement not only served well (if rather clumsily, when examined closely) the quantitative imperative to *measure*, but it also provided research psychologists with a convenient rationale for availing themselves of the methods of statistical analysis that had been developed outside the discipline (e.g., through the work of Francis Galton [1822–1911] and Karl Pearson [1857–1936]); (cf. Porter, 1986) but were being incorporated into the field as part and parcel of the testing movement that found its home in the burgeoning sub-field of differential psychology (Lamiell, 2003). During this same period, experimental psychologists were gradually abandoning the original Wundtian, single-subject approach to experimentation in favor of the treatment group model so well-suited to the nascent statistical method of analysis of variance (ANOVA) (Danziger, 1987, 1990; cf. Rucci & Tweney, 1980).

A potential stumbling block here came to be recognized in the dual fact that (a) the arithmetic operations proper to the aforementioned statistical methods of analysis, most fundamentally addition and subtraction, are meaningful only if the quantities being subjected to those operations are defined on scales with, minimally, interval properties, and (b) outside the domain of psychophysics, such scales of measurement had yet to be convincingly established.

Finally, this practice would find justification in the notion that it could serve heuristically useful purposes even if it could not, strictly speaking, *yet* be fully justified analytically. As S. S. Stevens (1968) would eventually put it: "The widespread use on ordinal scales of statistics appropriate only to interval or ratio scales can be said to violate a technical canon, but in many instances the outcome has demonstrable utility" (p. 856).

In sum, it can be said that during the first few decades of the twentieth century, the prevailing conviction within psychology's mainstream that *measurement is the hallmark of genuinely scientific inquiry*, the quantitative imperative, was conveniently complemented by a conception of measurement according to which *anything is measurable*, that is, representable by assigning numerals to the objects or events of interest in accordance with some explicit rule. Coupled with the widespread embrace of methods for analyzing the numerical data statistically, mainstream scientific psychology seemed to have all that it needed by way of quantification to proceed in a genuinely scientific fashion. Over the course of these developments, the relegation of qualitative methods to the periphery of the discipline was inevitable.

Of course, the history just traced is much more nuanced than this sketch reveals. However, due to present space constraints, and in consideration of the extensive writings of Michell on this topic—writings that are mandatory reading for one who would achieve a fuller understanding of this matter— the highly condensed treatment offered here will have to suffice.

My concern in the next section of this chapter will be with historical developments in connection with measurement's handmaiden in the quantification of psychological science: statistical methods of data analysis. Measurement concerns the process through which the phenomena under investigation are represented numerically, while statistical analysis pertains to what is done with those numbers after they have been created. If what Michell has called the "quantitative imperative"—the insistence upon measuring, however feebly, that which one wishes to study—has been a major factor in the marginalization of qualitative methods in psychological research, it is far from the only factor, and might not even be the most significant one. On the contrary, and as shall be seen below, the widespread adoption of, and continuing widespread adherence to, population-level statistical methods as a means of achieving scientific insights into the dynamics of psychological phenomena has, arguably, been a force of still greater potency in this regard. So in addition to what Michell has called "the quantitative imperative," the widespread "statisticizing" of psychology has also played a major role both in relegating qualitative methods to the periphery of psychological research and, to a large extent still, keeping them there.

The "Statisticizing" of Psychological Research

The Establishment and Developmental Course of "Differential" Psychology

Given the enormous role that is played in contemporary psychological science by statistical methods for estimating population parameters (means, variances, co-variances), it comes as a surprise to many that such methods were *not* part of the original experimental psychology practiced by Wundt and his contemporaries in the late nineteenth century. On the contrary, and although, as noted previously, attempts at *measurement* were very much a part of the discipline, statistical methods of the sort commonly practiced today would have made no sense, because *individual "doings"* (sensations, perceptions, judgments, recollections, etc.), and not parameters of variables defined only for populations, were the phenomena of interest. Where statistical calculations were made, as, for example, in the iconic research on memory carried out by Hermann Ebbinghaus (1850–1909), all of the data on which the calculations were based came from the same subject (in the case of Ebbinghaus's work, the subject was Ebbinghaus himself, cf. Ebbinghaus, 1885), and the purpose of the calculations was to estimate errors of measurement, not parameters of variables defined for populations.

As Ebbinghaus's work clearly illustrates, the general experimental psychology of the Wundtian stripe was—and was known and explicitly referred to as—an *individual* psychology. It was, to be sure, an experimental psychology seeking knowledge of general laws, but the term *general* was understood to mean "common to all" (of the individuals investigated), and not "true on average," as in the modern, statistical understanding of general.

It must also be recognized that Wundt was a proponent not of just one but of *two* psychologies: the general/experimental/individual psychology just mentioned, and also the *Völkerpsychologie* (cultural psychology). While the former was, indeed, hospitable to efforts toward measurement, the latter was necessarily reliant on methods that would today be recognized as qualitative (see, e.g., Wundt, 1964).

It was against this very background that William Stern (1871–1938) described the advent of population-oriented statistical methods as follows:

> The Wundt-ian bifurcation of method—experiment on the one side, cultural psychology on the other—is no longer adequate. Since around the turn of the new century, psychology has witnessed the emergence of a new discipline the systematic foundation of which the author has recently sought to provide: the differential psychology. It is concerned not with the general laws of psychological life themselves, but rather with the differential manifestations of those general laws across age, sex, race, and peoples, as well as across temperament types, character types, levels of ability and intelligence, etc. And these new questions have resulted in a new orientation. It has been necessary to modify the experimental approach so as to make it possible to investigate large numbers of persons with respect to more complex psychological processes and characteristics. Experiments entailing psychological "tests" have been devised. This development has necessarily entailed the extraction of precise psychological findings from large-scale investigations involving a great many research subjects, and this in turn has meant that data acquisition procedures and statistical methods have made their way into our discipline.
>
> (Stern, 1914, pp. 414–415)

This "new form of experimentation," and the reliance on population-oriented statistical methods that accompanied it, formed the core of that new sub-discipline of scientific psychology that Stern had, in fact, played a prominent role in founding, and that he proposed to name "the differential psychology." Through his first book on this subject (Stern, 1900), and even more so through his second and decidedly more advanced treatment of the subject (Stern, 1911), Stern effectively founded the framework that would house all of the various forms of psychological testing that would be pursued throughout the twentieth century and up to the present day. In this sense, the words with which Hans J. Eysenck (1916–1997) appreciated Stern more than 50 years after Stern's death are valid:

> William Stern may be credited with originating the concept of differential psychology, and laying down some of the rules which should govern its methodology. He clearly argued for an empirical and statistical approach and for a separation from orthodox experimental psychology. He anticipated many modern developments, and ranks among the founders of our science.
>
> (Eysenck, 1990, p. 249)

However, the picture of Stern projected by Eysenck in this passage is highly one-sided (cf. Lamiell, 2006, 2010). In the first place, Stern fully understood and insisted upon the distinction between, on the one hand, knowledge about *variables* with respect to which individuals could be quantitatively differentiated and, on the other hand, knowledge of the *individuals* who have been quantitatively differentiated in terms of those variables. This distinction was explicitly discussed by Stern in the very 1911 text on which Eysenck (1990) based his woefully unbalanced characterization of Stern. Another point to be emphasized in this context is that throughout his professional life, Stern insisted that psychological science would always have need for the kind of knowledge that could only be acquired by means of qualitative methods.

Illustrative of Stern's convictions in this latter regard, convictions that are conspicuously unmentioned in most extant references to Stern's contributions to psychology (Lamiell, 2006, 2010), is a passage that appears in his 1916 discussion of IQ testing of children who are functioning at sub-normal levels:

> In [some] respects, feeblemindedness is a *qualitatively distinct* kind of intellectual development. . . . [The] genuinely *qualitative* particularities remain unexamined by the test. . . . Just as is true of normal children, where the investigation of intelligence types has its own significance over and above the investigation of intelligence level, so also is it necessary with children who are not normal to take into account *qualitative* abnormalities alongside the quantitative sub-normalities, and to ascertain the former through special methods of investigation. *The current inclination, prominent in America, to see in the test a single, comprehensive, and universally valid method is to be steadfastly opposed.*
>
> (Stern, 1916, pp. 16–17; brackets and emphasis added)

Arguing in the same vein a short 5 years later, Stern wrote:

> For the examinee in question, tests yield a number on the basis of which that examinee can be located somewhere along a quantitative scale, but which obscures things qualitatively peculiar to that individual. The results of direct observation (which, for Stern, required qualitative methods) cannot be quantified, but make possible a qualitative refinement of the psychological profile. For all of these reasons, the methods of direct observation of an examinee must always be used to supplement the test methods, and the former must be developed and refined with the same care as the latter.
>
> (Stern, 1921, pp. 3–4, parentheses added)

The Stern that shines through this passage is not at all the Stern projected by Eysenck (1990) in the quotation cited above, but it is very much the Stern whose methodological convictions are vividly exemplified and richly confirmed by Sabat's research on the experience of Alzheimer's disease (see, e.g., Sabat, this volume).

One of the most influential proponents of the "prominently American" view that Stern "steadfastly opposed" was E. L. Thorndike (1874–1949). In a book titled *Individuality* and published, coincidentally, in the same year, 1911, as Stern's *Methodological Foundations of Differential Psychology*, Thorndike (1911) explicitly advocated for an elimination of the distinction between quantitative and qualitative differences, arguing as follows:

> A quantitative difference exists when the individuals have different amounts of the same trait . . . A qualitative difference exists when some quality or trait possessed by one individual is lacking in the other. A qualitative difference in intellect or character is thus really a quantitative difference wherein one term is zero, or a compound of two or more quantitative differences.
>
> (Thorndike, 1911, pp. 4–5)

In effect, Thorndike was advocating in this passage for reliance on some numerical coding scheme whereby seemingly qualitative differences (e.g., male vs. female) could be represented quantitatively (e.g., by consistently applying a coding scheme of 1-s and 0-s). Thorndike's position was thus altogether consonant with the quantitative imperative in psychology discussed earlier, whereas Stern's position was not. Thorndike's views prevailed.

As it happens, Thorndike also adopted in his 1911 book a stance on the interpretation of the population-level inter-variable correlations that obviated the epistemic need, insisted upon by Stern (1911), for a differentiation between knowledge of variables marking *individual differences*, on the one hand, and knowledge of *individuals*, on the other. Specifically, in his discussion of the meaning of correlations between measures of two traits in a population of individuals, he argued that such a correlation "[indicates] the extent to which the amount of one trait possessed by *an individual* is bound up with the amount *he* possesses of some other trait" (Thorndike, 1911, p. 22).

If this assertion by Thorndike is valid, then, in effect, knowledge of variables used to differentiate individuals within a population just *is*, at one and the same time, knowledge of the individuals who have been differentiated by those variables. On this view, the epistemic distinction that Stern insisted upon becomes superfluous, and the need for a research scheme other than the correlational scheme for gaining knowledge about individuals, that is, that research scheme that Stern called "psychography" (see Stern, 1911, p. 18; Lamiell, 2003, pp. 46–49) disappears. Here again, mainstream thinking within the discipline followed Thorndike rather than Stern.

"Psychographic" studies of individuals, which in Stern's view would have to include knowledge that could only be gained through methods of what he called "direct observation," that is, qualitative methods, thus never gained a place of prominence within mainstream differential psychology. Instead, "differential" psychology became essentially synonymous with the correlational scheme for investigating non-experimentally produced differences between individuals within populations. It is precisely this scheme that Lee J. Cronbach (1916–2001) would refer to as "correlational" psychology in his historical and well-known discussion of scientific psychology's "two disciplines" (Cronbach, 1957).

The Paradigmatic Conformation of Scientific Psychology's "Two Disciplines"

Of course, in the early years, the differential *cum* correlational psychology discussed above would, of necessity, remain independent of the existing experimental psychology for the reason already noted: The latter was devoted strictly to the investigation of individual-level "doings"—sensations, perceptions, judgments, etc.—while the sights of the former were trained on statistical estimates of parameters defined only for populations. For as long as this state of affairs remained in place, a merger of psychology's "two disciplines," *à la* the plea eventually issued by Cronbach (1957) would have been utterly impossible.

However, during the 1920s and 1930s, the original Wundtian model for experimental psychology was gradually forsaken in favor of a very different form of psychological experimentation referred to by Danziger (1990) as the *treatment group* method. In its most basic form this method entails sampling research participants (long called "subjects") from populations, assigning each at random to one of at least two treatment conditions defining the "independent" variable (IV), registering the performance of each participant as a score on some "dependent" variable (DV), computing the DV means and variances for each treatment group, and then comparing those treatment group means in search of evidence that there is a "statistically significant" difference between them, that is, a difference larger than would have been expected by chance alone given the within-group ("error") variances. Finding such a difference is taken as legitimate grounds for refuting the "null" hypothesis of no difference between the treatment group means, and for concluding that the difference obtained was produced by the differential treatment of the two (or more) experimental groups.

Extensions of this basic approach to experimentation so as to incorporate two or more IVs and multiple DVs could readily be accommodated by the refinement of that statistical technique known as ANOVA (cf. Rucci & Tweney, 1980), and this opened up possibilities for an experimental psychology vastly different from the discipline that had been initiated by Wundt and his late-nineteenth-century contemporaries. It also paved the way for the merger of experimental and correlational psychology eventually urged by Cronbach (1957), because once this transformation of experimental psychology had taken hold, the project within each of psychology's two disciplines was essentially the same: the search for statistically significant relationships between variables defined quantitatively for populations. That some of those relationships might be attributable to deliberate manipulations on the part of experimenters, thus (putatively) permitting causal inferences, while other relationships might be ambiguous with respect to causation was not a serious problem so long as the distinction between these two types of relationships remained recognized. Moreover, and as Cronbach (1957) argued, the breadth and complexity of the questions that psychological researchers could ask could be greatly expanded relative to what was feasible with Wundtian-style experimentation.

It goes almost without saying that the united discipline envisioned by Cronbach (1957), in which experimental and correlational investigations would be coordinated, is very much the core paradigmatic reality of what is today recognized as scientific psychology. In this incarnation, the discipline has become thoroughly statisticized, and there has been no place left to qualitative methods except at the field's periphery.

The Elephant in the Room

As explained above, the mainstream scientific psychology that is in place today is, from a methodological standpoint, a discipline in which knowledge claims are being tied not to empirical results obtained with individual subjects, as was the case in the original experimental psychology, but to the results of statistical analyses of population parameters: most fundamentally means, variances, and co-variances. This collective endeavor conforms to the original knowledge objective of psychology—the advancement of our ability to scientifically grasp the psychological "doings" of *individuals*—only on the presumption that the population-level knowledge that is actually generated by researchers in the field serves as a "window" of sorts into the dynamics of individual-level doings. Worrisomely, one searches in vain through the contemporary research methods textbooks for some thorough and compelling defense of this presumption (cf. Lamiell, 2016). Indeed, the present author has encountered only one text in which the presumption is accorded any discussion at all.

That text is a book authored by the estimable research methodologist Fred N. Kerlinger under the title *Behavioral Research: A Conceptual Approach* (Kerlinger, 1979). In that book, Kerlinger identified what he termed a "troublesome paradox," built into received thinking about how to properly conduct psychological research. The paradox is, he stated, "that scientists, especially psychological scientists, *must* hypothesize and test relations at the *group* or set level when they in fact often want to talk (theoretically) on the individual level" (Kerlinger, 1979, p. 276, parentheses and emphasis added).

In labeling this apparent theory–method disconnect a "paradox," Kerlinger (1979) implied that a conceptual bridge between the group-level knowledge actually secured through conventional statistical methods, on the one hand, and valid claims to individual-level knowledge, on the other, might in fact exist. But Kerlinger neither articulated such a bridge himself nor did he point to other work(s) in which such a bridge had been fashioned. So while Kerlinger's (1979) discussion did draw attention to a rather consequential epistemic problem, it did not achieve any closure on the matter. Nor, to the best of the present author's knowledge, has any other author achieved this goal. Indeed, the matter is simply not discussed.

The question thus begs as to how mainstream thinking in twentieth-century scientific psychology, and now well into the twenty-first century, could have allowed this problem to persist. A work by Cowles (1989) offering an historical perspective on the use of statistical methods in psychology suggests an answer to this question. In that work, Cowles discussed how in the interpretation of their research findings, psychological researchers over the years have been routinely "blurring" (Cowles's word) the distinction between frequentist and subjectivist thinking about statistical probabilities. "Frequentist" thinking scrupulously binds probabilistic knowledge claims to the consideration of a *series* of events. As the British logician John Venn (1834–1923) pointed out in his 1888 book *The Logic of Chance* (Venn, 1888), claims to knowledge of the probability of a single event, for example, an isolated coin flip, are incoherent.

In contrast, where acquaintance with some population-level statistical finding(s) is the basis for a probabilistic statement about a single event (e.g., what the probability "is" of *this* coin flip turning up heads), that statement can properly be understood only as an expression of the strength of the speaker's *subjective belief* about that event. In asserting, for example, that "it *is highly probable* that Smith will do or experience X," where the verb *is* functions (inappropriately) to express a statement of fact about Smith, the speaker ought really to be saying words to the effect "I *strongly believe* that

Smith will do X." In this latter locution, the speaker's statement is, transparently and just as it should be, an expression of that speaker's belief about Smith, and not a statement of some objective fact about Smith.

Astonishingly, having pointed to the prevalence within the psychological research literature of this blurring of the distinction between *knowledge claims*, on the one hand, and *statements of subjective belief*, on the other, Cowles (1989) went on to suggest that an attitude of "who cares?" could be justified on the grounds that "very few" psychological researchers had expressed any concern about it over the years (see Cowles, 1989, p. 59)! Arguably, it is in this same disciplinary indifference to a fundamental conceptual problem where we find an answer to the question of how Kerlinger's (1979) "troubling paradox" could have been allowed to exist for so long. Collectively speaking, the discipline has simply looked the other way.

Through the decades-long and discipline-wide practice of conflating two quite distinct meanings of probability, mainstream scientific psychology has routinely allowed statements about individuals that, given their grounding in the speaker's acquaintance with population-level statistics, *should* be formulated as expressions of *subjective beliefs*, to take instead the form of claims to *factual knowledge*. To cite just one recent and quite vivid example of this, we find boldly displayed on the cover of the November 2016 edition of the American Psychological Association publication *Monitor on Psychology* a picture of a young African American boy, accompanied by the text: "*This* boy *would be* three times more likely to be placed on a gifted-education program if *he* had a black rather than a white teacher" (*Monitor on Psychology*, November, 2016, emphasis added).

The population-level statistical analyses on which this knowledge claim is based could not, in fact, have established anything of the sort about "this" or any other individual boy. However, if the epistemic conflation built into this claim is ignored, all seems to be in good conceptual order in mainstream scientific psychology's house. It is this shockingly deliberate disciplinary "ignore-ance," that protects the illusion that a bridge of the sort required to resolve Kerlinger's (1979) paradox has long since been securely established.

In fact, no such bridge ever has been or ever will be established. The logically irrefutable truth is that knowledge of variables marking differences between individuals just *is not* knowledge of *any* of the individuals who have been differentiated in terms of those variables, or, indeed, of any individuals anywhere, and this is true whether the differences are produced by subjecting different individuals to different treatments, as in experimental psychology, or "captured" in their already existing state by assessment devices (tests) of one sort or another, as in differential/*cum* correlational psychology. Recalling the earlier discussion of the differing views on this matter represented by William Stern and E. L. Thorndike, respectively, what all of this means, succinctly, is that Stern was right and Thorndike was wrong. It is therefore most unfortunate that in overwhelming proportions, mainstream thinking in psychology aligned itself with the views of Thorndike.

What Stern saw that Thorndike did not (or chose to ignore) is that variables marking differences between individuals *are not defined for individuals*. It is for this simple reason that a science geared toward the production of knowledge about such variables cannot properly be regarded as a science of individuals at all. Knowledge about variables marking individual differences is, quite literally, knowledge of *no one*. It is knowledge of populations, and a discipline devoted to the production of such knowledge is properly regarded not as a psychology but as a species of *demography*. Unless "psychology" is now to be understood as having abandoned its original scientific objective of advancing our ability to scientifically grasp the doings of individuals, it should be clear from these considerations that a "sea change" of the sort alluded to by Schiff (this volume, Introduction: Situating Qualitative Methods in Psychological Science) is not only coming, but is long overdue (see in this latter regard Lamiell & Martin, 2017).

***

Immediate Implications

The memo declaring psychology's reinvention as a variety of demography seems to have had a quite limited circulation to date. Pending a clear and very public proclamation of this change (and the question begs as to who would be authorized to issue such a proclamation), it seems advisable at this point to proceed in the conviction that *psychology* remains committed to its original knowledge objective of advancing our ability to scientifically grasp the psychological doings of individuals. With this in mind, it is to be hoped that the foregoing discussion will facilitate a widespread reconsideration among mainstream psychologists of qualitative methods of investigation as valuable—perhaps even indispensable—tools in the prosecution of the discipline's mission.

At a minimum, the speciousness of the argument that qualitative methods must be minimized, or eschewed entirely, so as to insulate the discipline against a putatively non-scientific subjectivity in the psychological interpretation of research findings has perhaps been made easier to see. To the extent that mainstream "psychologists" restrict themselves to the population-level knowledge claims that their research findings can actually warrant, their knowledge claims might well qualify as scientific, but they fail as psychology because they are not *psychological* at all, but rather demographic.

On the other hand, to the extent that mainstream psychologists insist on making individual-level interpretations of their population-level research findings, they are *themselves* actually propagating subjective beliefs that have been *disguised*, via what might be termed "slights of wording," as objective knowledge claims. Unmasking those claims, it is plain to see that they are not nearly as devoid of subjectivity as is pretended. Nor could they be. For when mainstream psychological researchers leave the domain of the aggregate where their empirical findings actually lie, they enter territory that those findings cannot reach. Recourse to statements of subjective belief, however cleverly disguised as empirically warranted knowledge claims, is the inevitable outcome.

These, then, are the epistemic realities with which scientific psychology must now, at long last, come to grips.

A Final Word

As the implications of the considerations discussed in this chapter become more clearly and widely seen, the need will perhaps also come more clearly into focus for a serious discipline-wide reflection on what it means to speak of a *scientific* psychology in the first place. Here, too, some historical/etymological reflection can be helpful.

The word for "science" in the language of the land where experimental psychology was born was (and is) *Wissenschaft*. The first part of this word, *Wissen*, is, in its nominative form, the word for "knowledge." The second part of *Wissenschaft* is rooted in the verb *schaffen*, which means "to do" or "to make" or "to create." In its broadest sense, therefore, "science" can be characterized as an activity devoted to the "*schaffen*-ing" of *Wissen*, that is, the doing or making or creating of knowledge.

Note that on this broad—and historically valid—understanding of science, there is no stipulation expressed or implied regarding the *kind* of knowledge to be "*schaffen*-ed" (cf. Wertz, this volume). Indeed, late-nineteenth-century German scholars drew distinctions according to which quite different kinds of knowledge would all be considered *wissenschaftlich* or scientific. Philosophers, after all, were regarded as scientists no less than were physicists.

Consider further in this connection the famous treatise authored by Wilhelm Windelband (1848–1915) titled "History and Natural Science" (*Geschichte und Naturwissenschaft*; Windelband, 1894/1998). In that work, Windelband identified two major categories of science: the *rational* sciences (*die rationalen Wissenschaften*), logic and mathematics, which had no specific empirical content, and the *empirical* sciences (*die Erfahrungswissenschaften*). Within the latter category, Windelband further sub-classified the disciplines into the *natural* sciences (*die Naturwissenschaften*), including physics, chemistry, biology, astronomy, and the *human* sciences (*die Geisteswissen-schaften*), including the humanities, i.e., literature, theology, philology, history, and so on. Just where psychology would properly be located within this scheme was the major question addressed by Windelband (1894). He argued that from the standpoint of its *methods*, psychology would properly be classified as a natural science, but from the standpoint of its *subject matter*, psychology would properly be placed among the humanities. The point to be emphasized in the present context is that under *either* of these two placements, psychology would remain a *science*—a discipline devoted to the "*schaffen*-ing" of *Wissen*.

As is well-known, the objective of Wundt and the early experimentalists was to prosecute the individual, general, experimental psychology on the model of the natural sciences, and that is the orientation that won favor and has remained dominant within the mainstream—even after the Wundtian commitment to individual-level experimentation was abandoned. What has also happened, however, is the rise to hegemonic status of the belief that psychology would *have* to be modeled on the natural sciences to be genuinely "scientific" *at all*. It is this narrow belief that became wedded to the quantitative imperative and to the statistical methods that, today, so dominate psychology and the other "social" sciences (*die Sozialwissenschaften, not* to be confused with the *Geisteswissenschaften*). A psychology prosecuted as a *human* science, and hence necessarily reliant to at least some extent on qualitative methods of the sort common in those disciplines, came to be seen, and is still widely regarded as, distinctly *unscientific*.

To the extent that the present chapter helps to unmask a bit of the mainstream psychology's scientistic pretentions and, in the process, to de-fang its rejection of qualitative methods of investigations on the grounds that those methods are "unscientific," perhaps some additional space will be cleared for an expansion of psychologists' understandings of what it means—and could mean—to prosecute the discipline scientifically. Certainly, our late-nineteenth-century predecessors would have found nothing at all categorically unscientific about the use of qualitative methods, whether alongside of, in concert with, or wholly apart from (epistemically appropriate) quantitative methods (cf. Slaney & Tafreshi, this volume; Wertz, this volume).

Finally, it is the view of the present author that if contemporary mainstream psychologists understood both their own quantitative methods and their own disciplinary history better than they do, they would be much more circumspect in the claims they attach to their quantitative methods, and commensurately more receptive to qualitative methods than they now are (and long have been), and that the discipline of scientific psychology would be decidedly better off for this.

References

Cowles, M. (1989). *Statistics in psychology: An historical perspective.* Hillsdale, NJ: Lawrence Erlbaum Associates.

Cronbach, L. J. (1957). The two disciplines of scientific psychology. *American Psychologist, 12*, 671–684.

Danziger, K. (1987). Statistical method and the historical development of research practice in American psychology. In L. Krueger, G. Gigerenzer, & M. S. Morgan (Eds.), *The probabilistic revolution. Volume 2: Ideas in the sciences* (pp. 35–47). Cambridge, MA: MIT Press.

Danziger, K. (1990). *Constructing the subject: Historical origins of psychological research.* New York, NY: Cambridge University Press.

Ebbinghaus, H. (1885). *Über das Gedächtnis* [On memory]. Leipzig: Duncker & Humblot.

Eysenck, H. J. (1990). Differential psychology before and after William Stern. *Psychologische Beiträge, 32*, 249–262.

Kerlinger, F. J. (1979). *Behavioral research: A conceptual approach.* New York, NY: Holt, Rinehart and Winston.

Lamiell, J. T. (2003). *Beyond individual and group differences: Human individuality, scientific psychology, and William Stern's critical personalism.* Thousand Oaks, CA: Sage Publications.

Lamiell, J. T. (2006). William Stern (1871–1938) und der 'Ursprungsmythos' der Differentiellen Psychologie. *Journal für Psychologie, 14*, 253–273.

Lamiell, J. T. (2010). *William Stern (1871–1938): A brief introduction to his life and works.* Lengerich, Germany: Pabst Science Publishers.

Lamiell, J. T. (2016). On the concept of 'effects' in contemporary psychological experimentation: A case study in the need for conceptual clarity and discursive precision. In R. Harré & F. M. Moghaddam (Eds.), *Questioning causality: Scientific explorations of cause and consequence across social contexts.* Santa Barbara, CA: Praeger.

Lamiell, J. T., & Martin, J. (2017). The incorrigible science. A conversation with James Lamiell. Interviewed by Jack Martin. In H. Macdonald, D. Goodman, & B. Decker (Eds.), *Dialogues at the edge of American psychological discourse: Critical and theoretical perspectives in psychology* (pp. 211–244). London: Palgrave-Macmillan.

Michell, J. (2003). The quantitative imperative: Positivism, naïve realism, and the place of qualitative methods in psychology. *Theory and Psychology, 13*, 5–31.

Michell, J. (2004). The place of qualitative research in psychology. *Qualitative Research in Psychology, 1*, 307–319.

Michell, J. (2011). Qualitative research meets the ghost of Pythagoras. *Theory and Psychology, 21*, 241–259. doi:10.1177/0959354310391351

Michell, J. (2016). *The problem of measurement in psychology.* Unpublished manuscript. Sydney, Australia.

Monitor on Psychology. (2016, November). Washington, DC: American Psychological Association.

Porter, T. M. (1986). *The rise of statistical thinking: 1892–1900.* Princeton, NJ: Princeton University Press.

Rucci, A. J., & Tweney, R. D. (1980). Analysis of variance and the 'second discipline' of scientific psychology: A historical account. *Psychological Bulletin, 87,* 166–184.

Stern, W. (1900). *Über Psychologie der individuellen Differenzen (Ideen zu einer 'differentiellen Psychologie').* Leipzig: Barth.

Stern, W. (1911). *Die Differentielle Psychologie in ihren methodischen Grundlagen* [Methodological foundations of differential psychology]. Leipzig: Barth.

Stern, W. (1914). Psychologie [Psychology]. In D. Sarason (Ed.), *Das Jahr 1913: Ein Gesamtbild der Kulturentwicklung* (pp. 414–421). Leipzig: Teubner.

Stern, W. (1916). Der Intelligenzquotient als Maß der kindlichen Intelligenz, insbesondere der Unternormalen [The intelligence quotient as a measure of intelligence in children, with special reference to the sub-normal child]. *Zeitschrift für angewandte Psychologie, 11,* 1–18.

Stern, W. (1921). Rechtlinien für die Methodik der psychologischen Praxis [Guidelines for a method of psychological practice]. *Beihefte zur Zeitschrift für angewandte Psychologie, 29,* 1–16.

Stevens, S. S. (1946). On the theory of scales of measurement. *Science, 103,* 677–680.

Stevens, S. S. (1968). Measurement, statistics, and the schemapiric view. *Science, 161,* 849–856.

Thorndike, E. L. (1911). *Individuality.* New York, NY: Houghton-Mifflin.

Venn, J. (1888). *The logic of chance.* London and New York, NY: The Macmillan Company.

Windelband, W. (1998). History and natural science (J. T. Lamiell, Transl.). *Theory and Psychology, 8,* 6–22 (Original work published 1894).

Wundt, W. (1964). *Elements of folk psychology* (E. L. Schaub, Trans.). New York, NY: The Macmillan Company.

2 Quantitative, Qualitative, or Mixed? Should Philosophy Guide Method Choice?[1]

Kathleen L. Slaney and Donna Tafreshi

Introduction

Despite the title of the current volume, in this chapter, we will have little to say in specific terms about how exactly to situate qualitative research in psychology. Rather, our aim is to take a few steps back and examine more broadly the relationships among method, methodology, and philosophy of science. More specifically, our interest is in examining the tying of specific philosophical traditions to so-called quantitative and qualitative research paradigms, respectively, and the methods that have been historically privileged within each. In service of this aim, we will highlight the broad strokes of the qualitative–quantitative methods distinction, the philosophical traditions that have been tied to each, and the "incompatibility thesis" (Howe, 1988) regarding the viability of mixed methods research. We then offer arguments against the coherence of the view that quantitative and qualitative methods are inherently at odds with one another because they are wedded to incompatible philosophical foundations. Finally, we make an appeal for the adoption of a pluralistic, tools-based methodology, within which research questions and aims serve a key role in informing and guiding methods choices and, as such, critical reflection becomes a core feature of all research in psychology.[2]

The Quantitative–Quantitative Methods Distinction

As many readers are no doubt aware, the 1980s were a somewhat tumultuous period in social research in which "fierce debates" occurred concerning the relative merits of quantitative and qualitative research methods (Wiggins, 2014). In psychology, quantitative methods have dominated throughout the twentieth and twenty-first (thus far) centuries. Qualitative methods, conversely, have generally been eschewed by mainstream psychological and social researchers who view quantification as a necessary aspect of science

(Gergen, this volume; Lamiell, this volume). However, in the 1980s, a series of debates were spurred on by researchers working primarily within education, sociology, and nursing (Wiggins, 2014) who questioned the adequacy of quantitative methods for conducting social research and argued that qualitative research constituted a more appropriate paradigm for the social sciences. This led to further disputes regarding the distinctiveness of the respective epistemologies underlying quantitative and qualitative research paradigms and the methods favored within each (Bryman, 2006). Many qualitative researchers took the position that quantitative and qualitative research are undergirded by inherently incompatible philosophies. Quantitative and qualitative *research* paradigms were seen to be embedded in, and thus largely informed by, contrary *philosophical* paradigms.[3] Whereas the quantitative research tradition was construed as inextricably wedded to the (naïve) realist ontology and objectivist epistemology of positivism, qualitative research was seen as deriving from a constructivist, relativistic ontology and critically interpretivist, hermeneutic, epistemology (e.g., Guba & Lincoln, 1994, 2005). Such incommensurability in the philosophical foundations of quantitative and qualitative research traditions was thought to extend to methods themselves, leaving little hope for reconciling the two research paradigms, thereby compelling social researchers to pledge alliance to one or the other faction (Onwuegbuzie & Leech, 2005; Wiggins, 2014).[4]

The ultimate fate of the paradigm wars is a point of some contention. Gage (1989, p. 4) described them in the late 1980s as having come to a "sanguinary climax." However, Teddlie and Tashakkori (2003) stated more recently that successful employment of mixed methods has "largely discredited" the view that research paradigms are inherently incompatible (p. 19). In an even stronger pronouncement, Bryman (2006) stated that the paradigm wars are over and peace has broken out (p. 113). Yet, elsewhere, Bryman (2008) contended that the term "paradigm wars" is not easy to pin down and there is no consensus as to which paradigms were involved, when exactly the conflict began, and whether there really has been a "cessation of hostilities" (p. 13). In the same work, he warned that despite the impression given by the growing popularity of mixed methods that the warring parties have made a truce, it would be wrong to portray the paradigm wars as having totally ceased. Rather, it might be more accurate to characterize the debates concerning the relative place and worth of quantitative and qualitative methodologies as having continued at a slow burn for the past several decades, with recent statements about mixed methods constituting a possible third research paradigm having once again begun to fan the fires of the earlier debates.

As noted, a central theme of the paradigm wars was the question of whether quantitative and qualitative research methods follow necessarily from specific philosophical commitments. At the heart of this issue is the view that method choice follows in a top-down manner from epistemological and ontological stances adopted within a research community (Morgan, 2007). From this perspective, method choices are nested within, and thus constrained by, conceptions of the nature of the relationship between the knower and the known, where the latter is further constrained, at least to some extent, by notions about the form and nature of reality. Guba and Lincoln's (1994, 2005) well-known descriptions of research paradigms (or "inquiry paradigms," as they refer to them) conforms to this view. According to these scholars, whereas experimentation and quantitative methods are nested within the realist ontology and dualist/objectivist epistemology of positivism and postpositivism, hermeneutical and dialectical methods are nested within the historical and relativist ontology and transactional and subjectivist epistemology of critical theory and constructivism. This view implies that ontological and epistemological commitments *necessarily* constrain the methods available to the researcher.

However, not all contributors to the paradigm wars endorsed a top-down conception of research paradigms. Onwuegbuzie and Leech (2005) have described three major schools as arising from the paradigm wars: purists (or "incompatibilists"), situationalists, and pragmatists. These categories are conceptualized as lying along a continuum, with purists and pragmatists occupying the poles and situationalists in the middle. Consistent with the top-down perspective, purist-incompatibilists posit that quantitative and qualitative methods derive from different ontological and epistemological (and, also, axiological, rhetorical, logical, etc.) assumptions about the nature of research (Bryman, 1984; Collins, 1984; Howe, 1988, 1992; Onwuegbuzie & Leech, 2005; Tashakkori & Teddlie, 1998). As alluded to above, within this camp, quantitative methods are typically described as being associated with positivist and postpositivist perspectives, while qualitative methods are often described as being associated with interpretivist, constructivist, or phenomenological epistemic stances (Onwuegbuzie & Leech, 2005). The implication, for purists, is that due to irreconcilable differences between the positivist and interpretivist ontological and epistemological stances, intractable problems arise for approaches involving a mixture of methods that seemingly adhere to opposing philosophical frameworks (Sale, Lohfeld, & Brazil, 2002). Importantly, purists do not necessarily claim the incompatibility of quantitative and qualitative research methods at the level of practice—multiple methods can and often are used together. Rather, the putative Achilles heel for the possibility of *fruitfully* combining methods comes mainly from incommensurability in the epistemological paradigms that underlie quantitative and qualitative methods. Thus, for purists, the incompatibility stems from the impossibility of meaningful interpretation of research involving a combination of quantitative and qualitative methods. Howe (1988) characterized the purist stance in terms of the "incompatibility thesis," which he defines as the view that "quantitative and qualitative methods are incompatible because of the different conceptions of reality, truth, the relationship between the investigator and the object of investigation, and so forth, that each assumes" (p. 12). As Guba (1987) somewhat infamously averred, "the one precludes the other just as surely as belief in a round world precludes belief in a flat one" (as cited in Sale et al., 2002, p. 50) and, as such, should not be combined within a single research endeavor.

Unlike purists, pragmatists hold that the quantitative–qualitative dichotomy is a false one. Pragmatists also hold that the connection made between positivism and the tradition of using quantitative methods, and between interpretivist philosophies and the tradition of using qualitative methods, are both non-necessary. In other words, for pragmatists, there are no logical grounds for connecting quantitative research to positivism (or postpositivism) and qualitative methods to constructivism (or phenomenology). Moreover, pragmatists tend to emphasize the centrality of research questions in making decisions about the relative utility of quantitative, qualitative, or a mixture of research methods (Bryman, 2006). As such, unlike purists, pragmatists have little faith that epistemological allegiances are important for doing actual research and thus tend to "[relegate] epistemological and ontological debates to the sidelines" (Bryman, 2006, p. 218). We will return to a discussion of pragmatism below.

Situationalists see both classes of methods (quantitative and qualitative) as having potential, depending on the specific research context, but as falling short of compatibilism in maintaining the view that quantitative and qualitative methods are based on different paradigmatic commitments (Onwuegbuzie & Leech, 2005). From this perspective, some research questions lend themselves to a quantitative approach, others to a qualitative approach, but the two classes of methods are seen as more "complementary" than compatible (Onwuegbuzie & Leech, 2005).

The paradigm wars and aftermath have promoted the bifurcation of quantitative and qualitative research paradigms. The primary message taken up by incompatibilists is that quantitative and qualitative research methods are inextricably tied to specific philosophical perspectives (especially epistemological stances) and that such stances constrain, and thus drive, method choices. In the remainder of the chapter, we present several grounds for rejecting the incompatibility thesis, in particular, the premise that decisions about methods should fundamentally be determined a priori by philosophical assumptions. We argue in favor of a pragmatic, tools-based account of methods within which the adoption of specific methods or combinations of methods is guided primarily by the purposes and aims of research but not divorced from consideration of ontological and episte-mological stances.

Is the "Problem of Incompatibility" Really a Problem?

Drawing on the works of Howe (1988), Biesta (2010), Onwuegbuzie and Leech (2005), and others, we question the feasibility of the incompatibility thesis on two primary grounds. The first is that the dichotomization of quanti-tative and qualitative "research methods" has been criticized for being far too simplistic, ambiguous, and unjustified (Allwood, 2012; Åsberg, Hummerdal, & Dekker, 2011; Biesta, 2010; Onwuegbuzie & Leech, 2005). Methods are not themselves qualitative or quantitative (Biesta, 2010), nor are research para-digms or the ontological and epistemological (and other) stances they encom-pass. Moreover, the term *methods* is itself imprecise and an inadequate unit of comparison, as it captures a complex and multifaceted set of practices, including design, data generation, analysis, and interpretation (Howe, 1988). It has been argued by some (e.g., Biesta, 2010; Allwood, 2012; Åsberg et al., 2011) that the quantitative–qualitative distinction is only applicable to data. However, given the different means of obtaining so-called quantitative data (and, in some cases, qualitative), even here the distinction calls for further refinement. Is a rating of "4" on a 5-point Likert response scale of a ver-bal item stem, for example, quantitative or qualitative? What about counts of instances of maternal sensitivity based on coding of videotaped interactions between mothers and their infants? Are interpretations of observed correla-tion or regression estimates qualitative, even though they involve numerical information? Such questions do not lend themselves to categorical answers, as the distinctions between qualitative and quantitative at the various stages of the research process often lie on continua and are not neatly sortable into non-overlapping categories (Tashakkori & Teddlie, 1998).

As with ambiguities in the meaning of the term *method*, the discourse relevant to the paradigm wars invokes many different senses of the term *paradigm*. In most cases, it is used to refer to an epistemological standpoint (e.g., objectivist or phenomenological); however, in other places, the term is used either more broadly (e.g., *worldview*) or more narrowly (e.g., shared beliefs within a research field; Morgan, 2007). Sometimes entire philo-sophical movements are characterized as paradigms (e.g., the "inquiry par-adigms" of positivism, postpositivism, critical theory, and constructivism described in Guba & Lincoln, 1994, 2005) and at other times quantitative and qualitative research traditions are themselves described as "method-ological paradigms" (e.g., Howe, 1988; Wiggins, 2014). Thus, it can be difficult to isolate exactly what the quantitative–qualitative incompatibility (or compatibility, for that matter) refers to.

The quantitative–qualitative dichotomy breaks down further when one considers the overlap and similarities among research traditions. For example, all rely to some extent on observational methods, use standardized means of data representation to safeguard against bias, involve data reduction, give meaning to data through interpretation, use methods to verify (or "validate") both data and interpretations given of them, and so on (Onwuegbuzie & Leech, 2005). One might counter that such similarities are superficial and thus relatively benign in the face of contrary ontological and epistemological foundations. This is a fair enough comment and may be true when comparing exemplars from different research traditions. However, it does not settle the matter of whether or not quantitative and qualitative research are themselves as homogeneous and share as little overlap in their philosophical foundations as is often presumed. As Allwood (2012) argued, heterogeneity within the qualitative research tradition also calls into question the quantitative–qualitative dichotomy by sorting into a single category design, techniques, and analytic strategies that may share little in common, for example, empirically oriented grounded theory and phenomenological or hermeneutic approaches. And, as noted, given the various means by which quantitative data (i.e., "measurements") are generated, analyzed, and interpreted, one might also question the homogeneity that is presumed to exist within the quantitative research tradition.

The second issue on the basis of which we question the authenticity of the incompatibility thesis concerns the different philosophies of science that have been attached to quantitative (i.e., positivism and postpositivism) and qualitative (i.e., hermeneutics and constructivism) research traditions. As noted, qualitative research has been characterized variously as being founded on interpretivist, constructivist, and phenomenological epistemologies. Although we grant that these epistemological stances overlap in important ways, they are not simply different labels for a single epistemology. Rather, they carry somewhat different implications for the kinds of phenomena they speak to, as well as for the approaches and methods that are employed to understand those phenomena (see Gergen, this volume, for further discussion of ontology and epistemology). Given the much greater heterogeneity within qualitative research, it is possible that there is also heterogeneity in philosophical commitments (or, at least, the extent of alignment some researchers using qualitative methods have with hermeneutic, constructivist, or phenomenological frameworks is not strongly articulated). Moreover, it is often presumed that quantitative research cannot be approached from the perspective of interpretivist epistemologies. However, researchers such as Westerman (2006) and Yanchar (2006) argued that quantitative methods *can* be used in contextual and interpretivist-based inquiry. In their view, quantitative methods are not necessarily tied to the tradition of positivism and adopting such a position would restrict researchers from fully appreciating the range of uses of quantitative analytic techniques.

Furthermore, although quantitative methods are most often attached to positivism (and postpositivism), positivism has been characterized in different ways within the debates on the quantitative–qualitative dichotomy. Positivism is often framed in very general terms—that is, in a "just the facts, please" kind of way, in the sense of privileging observational methods. At other times, positivism is used as a label for a cluster of ideas that do not necessarily go together. Such "paraphernalia" of positivism, as Bryman (1984) has called them, include a preoccupation with operational definitions, mechanistic and reductionistic explanations, objectivity, replicability (to establish laws), and causality. However, as Biesta (2010) argued, just because certain ideas may be associated with one or more aspects of what is, in reality, a complex philosophical doctrine encompassing the works of many philosophers, some of whom would agree on little, does not imply an endorsement of all of the ideas that have been associated with the more general doctrine. This may be especially true for working researchers, who might endorse elements of positivism (e.g., reliance on inferences based on observations, interest in generalities, as well as a tendency to embrace the "quantitative imperative" and "statisticism," as described by Lamiell, this volume) without intending to explicitly advocate for a philosophical doctrine per se. Furthermore, it is not always clear what kind of philosophical doctrine positivism is presumed to be. For example, although it is oftentimes presented as an epistemology, in their frequently cited chapters from the *Handbook of Qualitative Research*, Guba and Lincoln (1994, 2005) presented positivism as a much broader "inquiry paradigm," which encompasses not only the "epistemological question," but also the "ontological" and "methodological" ones. Construed in this way, positivism (and the other inquiry paradigms presented in Guba and Lincoln) is *presumed* to encompass not only philosophical stances on the nature of reality and of what can be known and how, but also specific methods that are already sortable into "quantitative" and "qualitative" categories. Finally, positivism—as the received philosophy of science—was long ago abandoned as untenable, thus raising the question of what is the actual target of the incompatibilist critique.

Another problematic idea, one that is central to the present work, is that the use of a given method or set of methods necessarily *implies* a given epistemological (or other) stance and that adhering to one or more philosophical positions necessarily limits one to a specific method or set of methods. Howe (1988) claimed that the incompatibilist idea that abstract paradigms determine research methods in a one-way (top-down) fashion is not sound. He countered that the relationship is bidirectional and that, in practice, differences between quantitative and quantitative data, design, analysis, and interpretation can be largely accounted for by differences in research questions and approaches to addressing them and not necessarily by philosophical incommensurability. Åsberg et al. (2011) also rejected the idea that philosophical doctrines themselves can be broken down into those with either qualitative or quantitative a priori assumptions. They further argued that although, at the most general level, positivist epistemology adheres to the tenet that knowable means observable, "positivism *per se* has no preference for quantitative data" (p. 413). What's more, many qualitative methods involve empirical observation and inductive inference, both of which are hallmarks of positivist and postpositivist frameworks. Despite this, we admit that the associations that have been made between positivism/ postpositivism and quantitative methods and between interpretativism/ constructivism/phenomenology and qualitative methods are not spurious, even if philosophical commitments are often more implicit than explicit in practiced research. We also acknowledge that there is an important historical context in which such alliances must be understood and evaluated (see both Lamiell & Gergen, this volume) and that researchers should not view methods as being entirely devoid of theoretical and conceptual frameworks; indeed, such frameworks should be critically reflected upon and examined (Yanchar & Williams, 2006). Nevertheless, the primary issue we wish to question here is the validity of dichotomizing methods in terms of philosophical commitments in the way they often are in the discourse on research paradigms. We shall return to this point in the next section.

Despite the emphasis on epistemology, and more generally, philosophical commitments, in the paradigm debates, it is unclear whether the centrality of epistemological stance translates in a direct way to research as it is lived and practiced (Morgan, 2007; see also Gergen, this volume). For instance, not all, but many, researchers seem to be largely unaware of their philosophical position (Howe, 1992), and, by what they do and say, align themselves (intentionally or unintentionally) with multiple philosophical perspectives. That is, researchers, perhaps more in mainstream psychology than in other domains of social research, appear to be philosophically agnostic (or, at least, naïve). As such, it is quite possible that their methods choices are driven less by explicit philosophical commitments and more by conformity to established norms and conventions and shared sets of general beliefs within the research communities in which they work (Morgan, 2007). For instance, it is likely that many psychological researchers rely on measurement and statistics because these have been the only methodological tools presented to them during their training (largely for reasons outlined by Lamiell, this volume; see also Wertz, this volume). Thus, their use of quantitative methods may have less to do with truly believing—on epistemological grounds—that they are superior to methods used in qualitative research traditions than with conventions and, perhaps, a lack of awareness as to the range of methodological (and philosophical!) options open to them.[5]

In Defense of a Tool-Based Account of Psychological Methods

Based on the above points, we contend that the incompatibility thesis rests on weak intellectual footing and that there is a possibility of meaningful interplay between quantitative and qualitative research traditions within the field of psychology. In fact, Howe (1988) contended that, at least at the level of research practice, it is impossible to distinguish quantitative from qualitative, and thus quantitative and qualitative methods must be to some degree compatible. We advocate Howe's (1988) "compatibility thesis," which holds that combining quantitative and qualitative methods can indeed be beneficial to social research and that such a wedding of methods does not necessarily lead to epistemological incoherence. More generally, we advocate the view that methods, although undeniably related in complicated ways to the philosophical stances that operate within research domains, might be usefully thought of as tools. Moreover, some tools will be more useful for addressing certain kinds of research aims. The process of choosing a method is likely to be *influenced* by a researcher's philosophical presuppositions, but it need not be *constrained* by them. As such, we believe that a tools-based approach to method choice can accommodate the different kinds of inquiries in which psychological researchers engage, and also provides, where appropriate for the research question at hand, a coherent framework for combining quantitative and qualitative methods.

What Do We Mean by a Tools-Based Account?

We advocate a tools-based methods approach for psychological research based on two lines of argument. The first concerns the adoption of pragmatism as a foundation for research practice. Of course, the term *pragmatism* in the absence of qualification is somewhat vague. In the current context, it might be useful to distinguish *philosophical* pragmatism from *methodological* pragmatism, the latter of which shares close connections to what have been variously called *methodological pluralism* and *methodological eclecticism* (Wiggins, 2011). Construed in broad terms, philosophical pragmatism (the roots of which lie in the respective works of Charles Sanders Peirce, William James, and John Dewey) emphasizes that assessment of the "truth" of a statement or rightness of a decision or action is justifiable by the consequences of the thoughts, beliefs, and actions that prevail in light of those statements, decisions, and actions. That is, that which is the most effective (i.e., whatever "works best") is the primary criterion by which pragmatists judge the meaning, value, and significance of a proposition, belief, or action. Methodological pluralism and methodological eclecticism, although in most cases informed by a pragmatic philosophical orientation, tend to describe more of a general openness to adopting a range of approaches and methods in conducting research (Bryman, 2006; see also Gergen, this volume). We embrace both philosophical pragmatism and methodological pragmatism in the tools-based account we promote.

With respect to the former, we see pragmatism as providing not a specific set of philosophical *commitments*, but a general orientation to what issues need to be emphasized when articulating the aims and objectives of research and, then, making decisions about which methods will be employed. Within the pragmatic framework, knowledge is seen as acquired through a combination of action and reflection (Biesta, 2010). Importantly, philosophical pragmatism does not deny that researchers hold specific views about the world and of how knowledge is attained. Rather than providing a "paradigmatic underpinning or wholesale justification of mixed methods research" (Biesta, 2010, p. 97), pragmatism provides a set of philosophical tools that can be used to examine the connections between philosophical commitments and research methods and to address the specific problems with which a given piece of research, or a body of research, is concerned. It also provides a challenge to dichotomized thinking about philosophical commitments in research and allows for the possibility that researchers from different research traditions can engage in shared meanings and joint action (Johnson & Onwuegbuzie, 2004; Morgan, 2007).

Philosophical pragmatism manifests as methodological pragmatism most clearly in the view that researchers should choose the best method or combination of methods for satisfying the aims of the research at hand. This encompasses two main ideas. The first is that no method is ruled out a priori (Gergen, Josselson, & Freeman, 2015). The second is that method choices should be driven primarily by research questions, purposes, and the kinds of inferences researchers *really* wish to make as opposed to allegiance to specific philosophical or methodological traditions, or unreflective scientism (Biesta, 2010; Bryman, 2006; Johnson & Onwuegbuzie, 2004; Onwuegbuzie & Leech, 2005; Slife & Gantt, 1999; see also Lamiell, this volume). Indeed, quantitative methods are often useful for answering questions dealing with amounts, frequency, and magnitude, while qualitative methods tend to focus on questions of "what" and "how" (Wertz, this volume). Methodological pragmatism encourages researchers to consider the kinds of questions they ask and thus "prioritizes the research question and relegates epistemological and ontological debates to the sidelines" (Bryman, 2006, p. 118). Tashakkori and Teddlie (1998) frame this—somewhat facetiously—as the "dictatorship of the research question" (p. 20).

Of course, the adoption of pragmatism—philosophical or methodological—as a foundation for method choice is not beyond critique. Some have questioned whether it might simply be substituting one set of a priori philosophical assumptions with another (Biesta, 2010). Others have questioned whether a pragmatic approach to research really addresses head-on the issue of how to integrate philosophical (i.e., ontological and epistemological) worldviews (e.g., Slife & Williams, 1995; Stam, 2006; Wiggins, 2011, 2014). Concerns about the possible negative outcomes of advocating mixed methods have also been identified, for instance, when a combination of qualitative and quantitative methods is proposed but through a single unacknowledged worldview (Wiggins, 2011). We grant that these are important issues that will not simply be dissolved if pragmatism were to be adopted as a methodological framework for psychology. However, we also believe that pragmatism provides exactly the kind of philosophical and methodological middle-ground position (Johnson & Onwuegbuzie, 2004, p. 17) that such critical examinations of methods call for. The tool-based account of methods we envision begins with critical reflection about the specific phenomenon at hand (the ontological "space"), the nature of the relation between knower and known (epistemological stance) in the context of that phenomenon, as well as the possible value implications of research questions and proposed methods for addressing them (axiological considerations). Only then, in our view, can researchers choose reasonably and appropriately from a broad range of methods those that will "work best" for addressing research questions within the practical constraints at hand. This is the spirit in which we endorse pragmatism.

The second basis for the endorsement of a tool-based account specifically for psychology concerns the pluralistic nature of psychological subject matter (or, better, subject matters). Psychology is both ontically and epistemically plural and, as such, requires a broad and flexible methodology and set of methods (see both Wertz and Schiff, this volume). Psychology concerns itself with many kinds of "things" and multiple senses (uses) of "real" and "reality." Does it not then make sense that methods would also vary according to the specific nature of the "things" under consideration, but also, according to what a specific study aims to achieve? Moreover, psychologists and other social researchers, like all persons, are self-interpreting creatures; thus, among other things, they carry the burden of having to interweave axiological considerations into their theory and praxis. Such pluralism in the subject matters of psychology can only be adequately accommodated by a sufficiently rich and textured methodological pluralism. A tools-based approach thus not only opens possibilities for the kinds of tools psychologists might employ, but also for implementing important research principles for which there has been little room within the current methodological hegemony. This includes critical reflection, consideration of participants' perspectives, the role of researchers in knowledge construction, and the implications of research findings for social change. Given that many psychological researchers do not currently reflect on the philosophical dimensions of research, adopting a tools-based account in psychology is likely to promote not only a larger class of methods from which to choose, but also more critical reflection on the part of researchers regarding the methods choices they make.

***

A primary objective of the present chapter has been to push back against misleading and, often, unhelpful dichotomies (i.e., quantitative/qualitative, positivism/interpretivism, etc.) and the idea that philosophical positions *necessarily* commit researchers to using specific research methods and approaches. We also appeal for the adoption of a tools-based account of methods for psychology inspired by a pragmatic orientation. In so doing, we encourage critical reflection on method choice and method use in the context of the overall purpose of the research at hand. This would involve researchers questioning the utility of various methodological tools at different stages of the research process. For example, in the beginning stages, one might ask whether quantification of qualitative information using psychological tests will be fruitful for their research aims or if qualitative (non-numerical) representation of information will be more informative. As noted by Schiff in the introductory chapter of this volume, although quantitative representations of psychological phenomena might be useful in some instances, such representations also come along with many limitations, one of these being methodological reductionism. Indeed, both Schiff (this volume) and Sabat (this volume) nicely illustrate this point with examples of how non-quantitative representations of information capture an aspect of the relevant phenomena that quantitative representations are incapable of addressing.

We wish to be clear that we are not advocating that all psychological research necessarily must employ qualitative or mixed methods. Nor are we advocating an "anything goes" or "pick and choose" relativism where methods choices are concerned (Slife & Gantt, 1999). Rather, we are promoting the idea that certain kinds of methods (classified variously as quantitative, qualitative, or mixed) might be more appropriate than others for answering specific kinds of research questions. We also contend, along with the other contributors of this volume, that qualitative and mixed methods might be more successful in answering at least some research questions that have traditionally been explored in psychology using quantitative methods. Although we suspect that many research questions in psychology would probably benefit greatly from an eclectic approach, whether one adopts a single method or a combination of methods will be contingent to a large extent on the research question(s) and purpose(s) at hand. It will depend, if you will, on what "work" the research is intended to do. Sabat's (this volume), Wertz' (this volume), and Schiff's (this volume) chapters provide excellent examples of how methods may be coherently tied to specific research objectives. Moreover, we acknowledge Yanchar, Gantt, and Clay's (2005) point that *all* methods, whether quantitative or qualitative, are limited in the sense that they "enable certain types of understanding while foreclosing on others" (p. 28). According to Yanchar et al. (2005), this means that methods should constantly be reflected upon, revised, and advanced and that theoretical exploration is an important part of such critical reflection. We would add, however, that we do not believe that a certain type of method is *necessarily* tied to or constrained by a specific theoretical framework.

Clearly, there are also limitations and potential barriers to implementing a tool-based approach that is open to mixing methods, such as managing resistance to challenging the dominant philosophical and methodological hegemony (which we admit remains heavily entrenched in a naturalist, objectivist, ahistorical, and largely uncritical framework); contending with theoretically different ontological and epistemological stances; and implementing and training in a broad set of research practices (see Campbell, Gregory, Patterson, & Bybee, 2012). We acknowledge these and other challenges, but also note that such problems are neither new nor are they exclusive to mixed methods. In fact, we echo the views of Slife and Gantt (1999), Kirschner (2006), and Gergen (this volume) that methodological pluralism, if informed by a critically pragmatic philosophical orientation, may provide an impetus for psychology to examine its methodological assumptions and thereby promote a deeper understanding of problems with the methods that have been privileged and, hopefully, greater freedom to develop new and innovative methods.

Notes

1. Portions of the current work were presented as part of a collaborative programming symposium titled, "Situating Qualitative Research in Psychological Science" held at the American Psychological Association Annual Convention in Denver, CO, in August 2016.
2. A form of critical reflection referred to as "reflexivity" is a core principle in the tradition of qualitative methodology. Our use of the term *reflection*, in which researchers are encouraged to reflect on their role in the research process,

overlaps with the concept of *reflexivity*; however, we emphasize critical reflection somewhat more narrowly with respect to one's philosophical commitments and the practical utility of methods used within a study. This includes critical reflection on the constructivist/interpretivist framework within which the notion of reflexivity is embedded.

3. However, as Morgan (2007) and others have noted, what has been taken to constitute a paradigm is considerably more finessed. Morgan (2007) describes four versions of paradigms: worldviews, epistemological stances, shared beliefs in a research field, and specific model exemplars. The senses invoked in the current work conform primarily to the first two versions.

4. Bryman (2006) notes that the terms of the paradigm wars were set primarily by advocates of qualitative researchers, possibly because drawing out a distinct philosophical position for qualitative research provided an intellectual rationale for working outside of the hegemony of quantitative research. Researchers working within the quantitative research tradition, on the other hand, tended not to become so "entangled" in the demarcation of different philosophical traditions. Given the stronghold of the quantitative research within psychology, it is perhaps also not terribly surprising that psychology remained to a large extent unscathed by the paradigm wars (Wiggins, 2014).

5. A similar argument could be made regarding researchers working in domains where primarily qualitative methods are used. However, because qualitative researchers have had to fight to legitimize their modes and methods of inquiry, they are perhaps more inclined to examine their philosophical stances with respect to the phenomena under study. Nonetheless, it certainly is possible that methods choices made by some so-called qualitative researchers might also be guided primarily in accordance with convention rather than by philosophical commitments.

References

Allwood, C. M. (2012). The distinction between qualitative and quantitative research methods is problematic. *Quality and Quantity, 46*, 1417–1429.

Åsberg, R., Hummerdal, D., & Dekker, S. (2011). There are no qualitative methods— nor quantitative for that matter: The misleading rhetoric of the qualitative— quantitative argument. *Theoretical Issues in Ergonomic Science, 12*, 408–415.

Biesta, G. (2010). Pragmatism and the philosophical foundations of mixed methods research. In A. Tashakkori & C. Teddlie (Eds.), *Handbook of mixed methods research for the social & behavioral sciences* (2nd ed., pp. 95–118). Thousand Oaks, CA: Sage Publications.

Bryman, A. (1984). The debate about quantitative and qualitative research: A question of method or epistemology? *The British Journal of Sociology, 35*, 75–92.

Bryman, A. (2006). Paradigm peace and the implications for quality. *International Journal of Social Research Methodology, 9*, 111–126.

Bryman, A. (2008). The end of the paradigm wars? In P. Alasuutari, L. Bickman, & J. Brannen (Eds.), *The Sage handbook of social research methods* (pp. 13–25). London: Sage Publications.

Campbell, R., Gregory, K. A., Patterson, D., & Bybee, D. (2012). Integrating qualitative and quantitative approaches: An example of mixed methods research. In L. A.

Jason & D. S. Glenwick (Eds.), *Methodological approaches to community-based research* (pp. 51–68). Washington, DC: American Psychological Association.

Collins, R. (1984). Statistics versus words. In R. Collins (Ed.), *Sociological theory* (pp. 329–362). San Francisco, CA: Jossey-Bass.

Gage, N. (1989). The paradigm wars and their aftermath: A 'historical' sketch of research and teaching since 1989. *Educational Researcher, 18*(7), 4–10.

Gergen, K. J., Josselson, R., & Freeman, M. (2015). The promises of qualitative inquiry. *American Psychologist, 70*, 1–9.

Guba, E. G., & Lincoln, Y. S. (1994). Competing paradigms in qualitative research. In N. K. Denzin & Y. S. Lincoln (Eds.), *Handbook of qualitative research* (pp. 105–117). Thousand Oaks, CA: Sage Publications.

Guba, E. G., & Lincoln, Y. S. (2005). Paradigmatic controversies, contradictions, and emerging confluences. In N. K. Denzin & Y. S. Lincoln (Eds.), *Handbook of qualitative research* (3rd ed., pp. 191–215). Thousand Oaks, CA: Sage Publications.

Howe, K. R. (1988). Against the quantitative-qualitative incompatibility thesis or dogmas die hard. *Educational Researcher, 17*(8), 10–16.

Howe, K. R. (1992). Getting over the quantitative-qualitative debate. *American Journal of Education, 100*, 236–256.

Johnson, R. B., & Onwuegbuzie, A. J. (2004). Mixed methods research: A research paradigm whose time has come. *Educational Researcher, 33*(7), 14–26.

Kirschner, S. R. (2006). Psychology and pluralism: Toward the psychological studies. *Journal of Theoretical and Philosophical Psychology, 26*, 1–16.

Morgan, D. L. (2007). Paradigms lost and pragmatism regained: Methodological implications of combining qualitative and quantitative methods. *Journal of Mixed Methods Research, 1*, 48–76.

Onwuegbuzie, A. J., & Leech, N. L. (2005). On becoming a pragmatic researcher: The importance of combining quantitative and qualitative research methodologies. *International Journal of Social Research Methodology, 8*, 375–387.

Sale, J.E.M., Lohfeld, L. H., & Brazil, K. (2002). Revisiting the quantitative-qualitative debate: Implications for mixed methods research. *Quality & Quantity, 36*, 43–53.

Slife, B. D., & Gantt, E. E. (1999). Methodological pluralism: A framework for psychotherapy research. *Journal of Clinical Psychology, 55*, 1453–1465.

Slife, B. D., & Williams, R. N. (1995). *What's behind the research? Discovering hidden assumptions in the behavioral sciences.* Thousand Oaks, CA: Sage Publications.

Stam, H. J. (2006). Pythagoreanism, meaning and the appeal to number. *New Ideas in Psychology, 24*, 240–251.

Tashakkori, A., & Teddlie, C. (1998). *Mixed methodology: Combining qualitative and quantitative approaches.* Thousand Oaks, CA: Sage Publications.

Teddlie, C., & Tashakkori, A. (2003). Major issues and controversies in the use of mixed methods in the social and behavioural sciences. In A. Tashakkori & C. Teddlie (Eds.), *Handbook of mixed methods in social and behavioral research* (pp. 3–50). Thousand Oaks, CA: Sage Publications.

Westerman, M. A. (2006). Quantitative research as an interpretive enterprise: The mostly unacknowledged role of interpretation in research efforts and suggestions for explicitly interpretive quantitative investigations. *New Ideas in Psychology, 24*, 189–211.

Wiggins, B. J. (2011). Confronting the dilemma of mixed methods. *Journal of Theoretical and Philosophical Psychology, 31*, 44–60.

Wiggins, B. J. (2014). Mixed methods, overview. In T. Teo (Ed.), *Encyclopedia of critical psychology: Springer reference* (pp. 1195–1199). New York, NY: Springer.

Yanchar, S. C. (2006). On the possibility of contextual-quantitative inquiry. *New Ideas in Psychology, 24*, 212–228.

Yanchar, S. C., Gantt, E. E., & Clay, S. E. (2005). On the nature of a critical methodology. *Theory and Psychology, 15*(1), 27–50.

Yanchar, S. C., & Williams, D. D. (2006). Reconsidering the compatibility thesis and eclecticism: Five proposed guidelines for method use. *Educational Researcher, 35*(9), 3–12.

3 Qualitative Methods as Fundamental Tools

Autonomy and Integration in Mixed Methods Research

Frederick J. Wertz

This chapter explores qualitative research methods with a focus on their relationship with quantitative methods. A historical review suggests that measurement and quantitative analysis have undergone extensive development, whereas qualitative methods have been formally delineated and legitimized only within the last two decades. They have entered the curriculum relatively recently and remain to be integrated fully with quantitative methods. This chapter aims to contribute preliminary clarifications of the nature and relationships of qualitative and quantitative knowledge. The rich treasure trove of mixed methods research in the history of psychology is sampled, and recent guidelines are reviewed. Examples of advanced graduate students integrating qualitative and quantitative methods demonstrate diverse ways that integration addresses important problems in psychology.

Historical Perspective

During most of psychology's history, qualitative research methods have been viewed as lacking in rigor and of relatively little scientific value (Lamiell, this volume). Methods involving first person descriptive data, interviews, personal diaries, photographs, and creative products, as well as naturalistic observation and case studies, erroneously judged according to the goals and norms of quantitative methods, have been considered at best sources of hypotheses requiring measurement, aggregate quantitative analyses, and ideally randomized, controlled, experimentation (see, e.g., Lilienfeld, Lynn, & Namy, 2017). Qualitative methods have been assumed to produce knowledge serving the same goal as quantitative methods, causal hypothesis testing, and to be scientifically inferior to research designs featuring manipulation, measurement, and statistical analysis of variables. In the 1940s, Gordon Allport (1942) challenged these assumptions when commissioned by the National Research Council to investigate research using "personal documents" such as descriptions of experience, interviews, and graphic expressions—what is now called qualitative research in psychology:

> Strong counter-measures are indicated against theorists who damn the personal document with faint praise, saying that its sole merit lies in its capacity to yield hunches or to suggest hypotheses . . . they fail to express more than a small part of the value of personal documents for social science.
>
> (p. 191)

He called for "bold and radical experimentation" (p. 190) with these methods that would explore their full range of uses. However, it was not until the 1960s that qualitative methods began to be developed formally and were recognized as necessary tools to solve the problems of psychology. The word *qualitative research* was coined in the 1980s (Rennie, Watson, & Monteiro, 2001). Only in the last 20 years have these methods become widely recognized as producing a distinct kind of valid knowledge and placed in the curriculum (Wertz, 2014).

Qualitative understanding is deeply embedded and important in our everyday lives. We are familiar with human beings and how they are different from animals and physical things; the differences between perception, fantasy, and hallucination; the effects of trauma; and so on. We often need no special instruments or calculations to answer qualitative questions because we are capable, but by no means infallible, instruments. We use perception, recollection, comparative thinking, judgment, and communication with language in knowing the world qualitatively and using words to describe it. We often answer qualitative questions well enough, and even discover and overcome errors, without the kind of formal exactitude, certainty, and methodical practices of science. Qualitative understandings are so basic and ubiquitous in our lives that they are taken for granted. Whereas quantitative scientific practices have been extensively developed, the problems, issues, and norms of sophisticated qualitative knowledge have remained relatively obscure.

Methodological Fundaments

The evaluation of methods requires understanding the kinds of questions they answer. Quantitative questions concern magnitude and prevalence (frequency)—how much and how many. We can ask about changes in magnitude over time or differences between individuals and groups. Understandably much attention has been devoted to these questions, for they can be important, even matters of life and death. How much oxygen is reaching a patient's brain? How many people have been murdered in a city? The importance of quantitative knowledge, which depends on the exactness, certainty, and standardization that constrain and even appear to eliminate the investigator's subjectivity, has made it so attractive that psychology has universalized it, tried to translate all questions into quantitative ones and answer them accordingly.

Qualitative knowledge is not a simple matter. Qualitative questions concern *what something is*—how it is different from other things, including function, meaning, value, and purpose; constitutive aspects and how they interrelate; changes over time; consequences, sequelae, outcomes; and relations to related phenomena and contexts. Knowing *what* something is entails a conceptualization of the topic as a whole and in its various parts, the way these parts are related and organized, how it is similar and different from other things, and how it is related to surrounding matters. Knowing *what something is* includes its *how*—its process and temporal unfolding as well as its social context, including ramifications and significance in the larger world. To qualify as scientific, qualitative knowledge must be based on necessary and sufficient observations and analyses that produce conceptual fidelity to the observed in natural language expressions.

Because the construction of theories, predictive and explanatory hypotheses, and measurements of every sort require qualitative knowledge, its relative adequacy and scientific rigor matter. Like quantitative practices, qualitative methods can be done well or poorly and depend on sound procedures and norms. Although psychological research and theorizing may proceed with taken for granted, vague, misleading, and inadequate qualitative knowledge, research can also be methodical, self-critical, and offer adequate evidence. All empirical scientific research, qualitative and quantitative, can be flawed and improved over time and never achieve the finality, certainty, and indubitability of formal sciences like mathematics and pure logic.

Qualitative knowledge forms a necessary foundation of empirical quantitative knowledge inasmuch as measurement requires and presupposes what is measured. In and of themselves, numbers tells us only the *magnitude* and *frequency* of phenomena, not what they are. Even when many measurements are made with the most precise instruments and analyzed with the best statistical procedures, they do not provide knowledge of what is being measured and what the numbers mean. Quantitative knowing is necessarily based on and is impossible without qualitative knowledge, whereas not vice versa. Quantity is always a quantity *of something*, and a number representing magnitude or frequency in itself does not provide knowledge of what that something is. Because measurement is impossible apart from its qualitative substrate, the qualitative question of what is being measured is an important one. Without qualitative knowledge, we literally do not know what we are measuring in a fully scientific way. To the extent that psychology's knowledge is not based on qualitative methods, one can say that it is *not fully scientific.*

Qualitative knowledge is also required as a necessary interpretive context for quantitative knowledge. Numbers reflecting measurement represent an attribute of what is measured, and quantitative designations of *more, less, increase, a lot, a few* are predicates. *What*s require qualitative explication, determinations of meaning, value, and purpose. In other words, *larger* is a quality as well as a measured quantity. One dollar, one hundred dollars, and a thousand dollars are qualitatively different. Therefore qualitative questions and knowledge about quantities are important. An increase of body temperature of two degrees Fahrenheit from 98° to 100° is very different from an increase to 102.5° and 104.5°. The former usually signifies a fever that can be monitored at home whereas the latter two usually signify respectively a medical concern and an emergency. In qualitative matters, meaning, value, purpose, temporal and social contexts, and outcome are at issue. It is sometimes assumed that statistical significance means "importance," but importance to whom, with what importance, or for what purpose? The difference between means of experimental and control groups may be decisive primarily for the conventional practice of hypothesis testing or it may be of momentous significance and practical consequence. Questions concerning clinical significance, the personal and social importance, of a difference between means is a qualitative, not a quantitative, question. If we do not empirically know the meaning of quantities, our science is severely limited, especially when it is applied to situations outside the context of scientific research. Interpreting quantitative results requires qualitative knowledge.

To summarize the above two points of interrelation, the qualitative is more fundamental than the quantitative because (1) measurement is necessarily directed at a predetermined quality, and (2) empirical quantities require qualitative explication. Quantitative knowledge is therefore inextricably related to and requires qualitative knowledge. Often this knowledge has been lacking in psychology because rigorous qualitative methods to empirically address such questions as "what is being measured?" and "what is the meaning of the quantity measured?" have not been formally developed with the necessary norms included in our science education and generated in scientific research. Psychology's identification of science with quantitative methods and failure to recognize the fundamental importance of qualitative methods left a major gap at the heart of the science itself.

Important basic qualitative work has always been done in the physical sciences, for instance in charting the stars and planets in astronomy, developing classification systems for plants in botany, describing the structure and functions of organ systems, and differentiating the stages of embryonic development in biology. Such human phenomena as learning, intelligence, emotion, family relationships, education, and democracy, notwithstanding their familiarity in everyday life, require qualitative knowledge as sophisticated as our best measurement techniques and statistics to inform psychological research and interpret its results. Rigorous scientific methods are necessary for our knowledge of what psychological phenomena are in their structure, their temporal process, their contextual relations, and their significance. Psychology has many qualitative gaps to fill in its knowledge, and qualitative methodology has much catching up to do.

The Role of Qualitative Methods in Defining Psychological Subject Matter

Many debates in the history of psychology may be traced to the lack of scientific qualitative knowledge. Even today, there remains a significant lack of scientific knowledge of such basic phenomena as perception, learning, memory, thinking, motivation, development, personality, social life, and psychopathology. What is learning? Is it an increase in the frequency of behavior? What is intelligence? Is it IQ? What are human beings, the kind who participate in experiments? How do our psychological subject matters, research questions, constructs, operational definitions, measurements, and research results relate to their complex, multifaceted, reality? After all, qualitative questions of the nature of phenomena like learning and intelligence, indeed of the very nature of "persons," have been and continue to be matters of conflicting claims and controversy in psychology. Asking important qualitative questions and using careful, self-critical, methodical, and accountable procedures to answer them is crucial for our science.

The subject matter of psychology itself has been variously defined, for instance first as mental life, then as behavior, and more recently as the brain. The conceptual clarification of our subject matter is an important and fundamental issue, whose difficulties have in part led to its abandonment. The current breadth of subject matter diffuses, perhaps in unprincipled and inappropriate ways, into other disciplines ranging from biology to anthropology and even literary studies (see Sabat, this volume). From the beginning of psychology as a distinct science, we have been faced with the question of what mental life is and how we know it. This long-standing and fundamental qualitative question remains because of the disproportionate development of quantitative methods and of our lack of commitment to the development of rigorous qualitative methods, which has bequeathed a paucity of tools to solve these problems with procedures and norms of kind.

Qualitative analysis by philosophers of science and theoretical psychologists provide resources for qualitatively grounding and informing the science of mental life, including its quantitative research (e.g., continental philosophy and American pragmatism). These works converge on a general conceptualization of mental life as embodied, teleological, meaning finding/making, temporal, agentic, and social-cultural. Current interest in qualitative methods affords an opportunity to consider basic disciplinary questions and to answer them using philosophy, theory, and the developments within psychology itself (see Gergen, this volume). From these overarching disciplinary issues, we turn to the proximal topic: the integration of qualitative and quantitative methods in response to the scientific problems posed by psychological subject matter.

Three Historical Examples of Mixed Methods Research

A large and fascinating history of mixed methods research has been underappreciated and insufficiently studied. Research conducted prior to the establishment of scientific norms contain excellent practices that can inform the growing integration of qualitative and quantitative methods in textbooks, guidelines for grant proposals, and formal education.

Marienthal: An Investigation of Poverty

One wonderful example is *Marienthal: Sociography of an Unemployed Community*, first published in 1933 by Marie Jahoda, Paul Lazarsfeld, and Hans Zeisel (2002). This study of poverty aims to fill the gap between the statistics, which the authors called "superficial," and unscientific knowledge from journalism and other anecdotal works. These researchers believed that social life could not be fully understood without a synthesis of statistics and a descriptive explication of the concrete life to which the statistics refer. Using interviews, observations, and photographs with statistics, they provide a "comprehensive picture of life in Marienthal" (Jahoda et al., 2002, p. 2), a German village that plummeted into unemployment and devastating poverty after its industry was dismantled in 1929.

The study was conducted in the University of Vienna's Department of Psychology, chaired by Karl Bühler, who hired Marie Jahoda, a psychologist (with 10 psychological research assistants). Paul Lazarsfeld, with a background in mathematics, physics, and the social sciences, provided the institute with statistical expertise and created its Research Branch for Economic Psychology with Bühler's encouragement and Rockefeller Foundation support. Zeisel's background in economics, law, and the history of qualitative methods completed the interdisciplinary team. Researchers lived in the community with compassion and social engagement, combin(ing) the use of numerical data with immersion into the situation. To this end it was necessary to gain such close contact with the population of Marienthal that we could learn the smallest details of their daily life. At the same time we had to perceive each day so that it was possible to reconstruct it objectively; finally, a structure had to be developed for the whole that would allow all the details to be seen as expressions of a minimum number of basic syndromes (qualitatively and quantitatively represented structures of poverty).

(Jahoda et al., 2002, pp. xxxv–xxxvi, parentheses added)

In 1932, Lazarsfeld presented the findings at the International Congress of Psychology and, in 1933, the team published a report in German. In a faculty position at Columbia University shortly thereafter, he began translating the report into English and wrote a paper on its integrative methodology. However, he did not publish the manuscript at that time because these methods were so incompatible with those he was teaching his graduate students. The report appeared in English only in 1971, with Lazarfeld's work on its mixed methods research methodology included as the Foreword. The Afterword, written by Zeisel, provides an invaluable history of mixed methods from the Middle Ages through the twentieth century.

Moral Reasoning

In his outstanding 1958 doctoral dissertation, Kohlberg (1994) used mixed methods to study the development of moral reasoning. Kohlberg's investigation was made possible by the interdisciplinary milieu of the University of Chicago. His mentor, sociologist Anselm Strauss (a former Columbia student of Paul Lazarfeld), introduced Kohlberg to the richness and rigor of qualitative methods before developing grounded theory with Bernie Glaser (Glaser & Strauss, 1967). Kohlberg collected children's reasoning about hypothetical moral dilemmas in 2-hour tape-recorded interviews and in focus groups where participants attempted to agree on resolutions of morally challenging situations. Kohlberg used ideal typological methods (Weber, 1949) to formulate qualitatively distinct cognitive structures from the mass of verbal data. He found three major types, each differentiated into two sub-types, yielding six structures of moral reasoning. Returning to the data, Kohlberg assigned each expression of moral thinking to one of the six categories, each classified along 30 dimensions, and organized data points in a grid of 180 cells. Because individual participants each expressed numerous types of reasoning, the percentage of each participant's statements in each of the six categories was determined, and participants were classified according to their modal response. Fifteen of the 72 children were found to be thinking modally on the first level. Kohlberg developed standardized procedures for measuring average levels of moral reasoning among persons of various ages. He went on to quantitatively investigate moral reasoning in many ways, including changes in type of reasoning over time, rates of reasoning development in various cultures, and the effects of intervention programs in prisons and schools (Kohlberg, 1971).

One of Kohlberg's most difficult problems was empirically supporting his conclusion that the six structures of thinking form a developmental sequence. Guttman's technique was used to quantitatively analyze their consistent age trends. A correlation matrix verified the sequential nature of the types in decreasing correlations among types that were hypothesized as less developmentally proximate to each other. Quantitative findings also indicated that from ages 10 to 16, earlier types of moral reasoning decreased and that more advanced types increased. Kohlberg considered the qualitative analysis and evidence of developmental sequence to be superior to the quantitative. "More strongly than the quantitative data, we believe that the qualitative data and interpretations contained in our stage descriptions makes the notion of developmental transformations in moral thought more plausible and meaningful" (Kohlberg, 1963, p. 19). Kohlberg presented evidence that new reasoning stages progressively encompass older ones in an orderly sequence; over development, new cognitive structures surpass and integrate previous ones resulting in new meanings of "right" and "wrong."

Kohlberg's research was published in *Vita Humana* in1963 as a short article containing virtually no description of his mixed methods. Only in 1994, well after Kohlberg's ground-breaking work shaped the field, were his mixed methods made available in a published photocopy of the original dissertation (Kohlberg, 1994). Despite the tremendous impact of this sophisticated research, very little attention has been devoted to Kohlberg's mixed methods (Wertz et al., 2011; Wertz, 2014).

Experimental Psychology of Learning

One final example of mixed methods research that has been obscured in the annals of psychology comes from the research program of Amedeo Giorgi who developed phenomenological research methods at Duquesne University in the 1960s. Giorgi and his students embedded qualitative methods within replications of experiments on learning. Experimenters collected written experiential reports from participants, detailing, for instance, the learners' experiences of stimuli (Colaizzi, 1967). Giorgi (1970) published one experiment on serial learning in which participants were instructed to remember pairs of non-sense syllables. He supplemented the quantitative results of experimental trials with rich descriptions of the strategies partici-pants used to learn the paired associates, including creative and effective uses of imagination to make meaning of and thereby to interrelate the non-sense syllables. This integration provided qualitative knowledge of what was being measured in experiments and delineated the mental processes that explained causal relations between stimuli and outcomes of learning. A psychology of learning that does not include the agency and experienced meanings of learned material misses the very subject matter of learning. In a follow-up phenomenological study, Colaizzi (1973) showed that some research, presumably on learning, does not study learning but only activities such as memorization that were previously learned.[1]

The Emergence of Mixed Methods Research: Integrating Disparate Traditions

One important recent development in psychology has been the sharp increase of qualitative and mixed methods research. Kazak (2018) reported a dramatic increase of articles with "qualitative" in the title in PsycNet, from under 200 in the mid-1990s to 3,000 in 2005 and cited a 3.8 fold increase from 2006 to 2016. In 2001, the National Institutes for Health's Office of Behavioral and Social Sciences Research (2001) reported the broad appeal of combining methods in public health research and offered assistance to researchers submitting proposals for federal support. In a 2010 study of NIH funded investigations, Piano Clark documented an increase over the last two decades in health-related mixed methods research, funded by 23 NIH insti-tutes, including the National Institute of Mental Health, the National Institute of Nursing Research, and the National Cancer Institute (Piano Clark, 2010).

In a white paper on mixed methods commissioned by the Office of Behavioral and Social Science Research, National Institutes of Health, Cres-well, Klassen, Piano Clark, and Clegg Smith (2011) define mixed methods and methodology as:

- Research that calls for real-life contextual understandings, multi-level perspectives, and cultural sensitivity
- Quantifying magnitudes as well as exploring the meaning of constructs
- Using multiple methods (e.g., intervention trials and interviews)
- Intentionally integrating methods to draw on the strengths of each

One of the benefits of mixed methods research is to bridge research meth-ods with different goals, strengths, and limits.

The choice of research methods is a complex process. Optimally, specific methods are chosen and employed in light of the researched phenomenon and the researcher's goal(s), but also with an understanding of how different methods are able to access different aspects of the researched phenomenon to achieve different goals. Diverse goals include discovery, theory generation, hypothesis testing, interrelating variables, practical action results, methods development, program design/evaluation, and larger issues of personal emancipation and social justice. This intertwining of phenomenon and aim can be seen in what Creswell et al. (2011) call the "targeted level" of research, for example, the individual person, policy, organization, family, community, or culture. The nature and full complexity of each research topic is not known at the outset of research when methods are initially selected. Although every project aims to access its phenomena adequately, research proceeds in critically considered steps and requires humility in the face of a reality that exceeds its knowledge. Research also operates within particular theoretical and philosophical traditions that themselves have distinctive goals, subject matters, and bodies of knowledge (Levitt et al., 2018). Some have assumed that qualitative and quantitative research methods are inextricably wedded to philosophies of science that are incompatible with each other (Slaney & Tafreshi, this volume). It can no longer be assumed that philosophies of science and theoretical traditions are incommensurate or irreconcilable; mixed methods research fruitfully demonstrates compatibility. Contemporary psychology is benefiting from theoretical, philosophical, and methodological pluralism (Gergen, this volume), and mixed methods research is also enhancing knowledge by integrating multiple theoretical orientations (Creswell et al., 2011). Science benefits from creativity unconstrained by philosophical systems (Wertz et al., 2011). Methods are most appropriately evaluated by their utility to achieve research goals with fidelity to the researched phenomenon.

Creswell et al. (2011) state that the strength of qualitative research is its focus on meaning, context, the voices of participants in natural situations, unknown phenomena, explanations of how and why phenomena occur, and the range of effects. They characterize quantitative research as most often focused on deduction, descriptive information, relationships among variables, population comparisons, and measurable evidence of causality. When research problems require both kinds of knowledge to achieve research goals, different methods can be integrated simultaneously, successively, or in alternation. In this way, they provide perspective enhancement, contextualization, more complete understanding, concrete illustrations of findings, understanding of processes and experiences, as well as outcomes—in short, a more complete data base (Creswell et al., 2011).

Yoshikawa, Weisner, Kalil, and Way (2008) have argued that the qualitative–quantitative distinction is somewhat arbitrary and limiting. Challenging overly simplistic conceptualizations of the contrast, they argue against the usual view of qualitative versus quantitative research: small versus large samples, ungeneralizable versus generalizable, non-causal versus causal, non-experimental versus experimental, and culture specific versus universal (p. 345). In a more nuanced view, they show how both words and numbers are necessary to understand causality. Quantitative methods estimate the direction and magnitude whereas qualitative methods uncover "mechanisms," detail the processes and temporal organization, including the crucial functioning of human agency that links treatment and outcome variables (see Schiff, this volume). They cite a study by Clampet-Lundquist, Edin, Kling, and Duncan (2006) that elucidates why moving to low-poverty neighborhoods had more positive effects on girls' than on boys' academic performance and social behavior. Qualitative analysis of in-depth interviews showed that girls, who felt more harassed and were more fearful than boys in their old neighborhoods, engaged more quickly and adaptively than boys in school-based friendship networks whose members were less likely to engage in high-risk behaviors (Yoshikawa et al., 2008). Note that the contribution of in depth interview data in this study was not limited to quality (engagement with friends, high-risk behavior,) but also revealed quantitative differences (engaged *more* quickly, *less* likelihood of risky behavior) between girls and boys. Contemporary integrations of qualitative and quantitative methods are teaching us that, even as distinctive as each may be, these two ways of knowing can be overlapping and inseparable (see Slaney & Tafreshi, this volume).

Integrating Qualitative and Quantitative Research in Advanced Education

Students with competency in multiple methods are increasingly able to employ the phenomenon-goal dialectic to address scientific problems in psychology.[2] The following research projects were conducted in Fordham University's, mostly, quantitative psychology department by students in clinical, developmental, and psychometrics-quantitative doctoral programs. The first and third examples show how qualitative research can be used to interpret otherwise obscure quantitative findings, and the second and fourth examples demonstrate the use of qualitative methods to inform quantification, respectively in test construction and mathematical modeling.

Qualitative Analysis Based on Measurement: Clinical Versus Subclinical Bulimia Nervosa

In a study on bulimia nervosa (BN), Skoufalos (2010) used a comparative phenomenological psychological analysis of interviews and focus group discussions to conceptually differentiate clinically diagnosable BN, subclinical BN (SCBN), and no BN (NBN). Previous research on BN had brought to light numerous risk factors and supported many etiological theories. However, knowledge of such associated factors as sociotropy, dissociation, and anger as well as such determinants as family, psychodynamics, behavioral and cognitive processes were unintegrated (see Schiff, this volume on variable-centered psychology). Researchers (e.g., Gleaves, Lowe, Snow, Green, & Murphy-Eberenz, 2000) debated whether or not SCBN, which involves binging and purging at frequencies too low to meet diagnostic criteria, is similar to BN and may lead to clinically diagnosable BN. Is the psychology of those binging less than three times a week different from those binging more frequently? By tracing the life historical development of BN and comparing it with those of SCBN and NBN, Skoufalos provided integrative knowledge of associated and etiological factors and of the similarities and differences between people classified as having clinical and subclinical BN. She used quantitative questionnaire items to identify three groups of participants who then participated in focus groups. To the researcher's surprise, phenomenological analysis (Giorgi, 1985) yielded three psychological structures: (1) deeply rooted experiences of loneliness, isolation, and personal emptiness with desperate and failing attempts at refuge in love and bodily comfort (BN); (2) suffering risks of rejection in close, affectionate relations with others when failing to meet uncritically adopted expectations of perfection (SCBN); and (3) acceptance of bodily and personal imperfections without risk of rejection (NBN). Although the general structures of both BN and SCBN included problematic family relationships, devalued body image, sociotropy, dissociation, feelings of anger, and binging/purging, each of these variables had very different qualitative meanings for the two groups. These findings resolved the debate, showing that SCBN is not simply a less severe version of BN at risk for progressing to BN, but involves a qualitatively different psychological structure. The two holistic qualitative descriptions of BN and SCBN provided more definitive, coherent, and comprehensive psychological knowledge by including personal goals and meanings within social, cultural, and developmental contexts.

Test Construction Based on Qualitative Analysis: Measuring Institutional Culture

Kathy Jankowski, Ann Higgins, and I employed qualitative methods to construct a test to measure the "Catholic institutional culture" of colleges and universities. Our approach was both top down and bottom up in that we analyzed the theoretical and educational literature relevant to Catholic education and conducted dozens of interviews with students, teachers, administrators, and staff. The integration of the documentary and empirical analyses identified six basic constituents of the institutional culture of Catholic higher education. We extracted 300 statements directly from the interviews to express them in participants' language. By eliminating redundancy, we reduced these statements to 100, with 16 items representing each of the six constituents/scales: Visible Links to the Catholic Church; Charism; Curriculum; Behavioral Norms; Personal Formation; and Multi-religious Culture. Multi-religious Culture was not found in the theoretical and educational literature yet was extremely salient in the analyses of the interviews, representing a relatively recent dimension of Catholic educational culture on the ground. Catholic universities are now places that welcome, support, and cultivate the development of Catholics and persons of all faiths and no faith—very different from the exclusive focus on Catholicism in the past. These 100 statements were transformed into test questions using a 5-point scale that could be administered to respondents concerning the their college or university. The next step in this research will be to pilot these questions and to conduct factor and item response analyses to assess the psychometric properties of the test items. The test will afford a measurement of Catholic institutional culture that is faithful to its multifaceted, complex, reality across various institutions and time.

Using Qualitative Methods to Interpret Quantitative Findings: Educational Psychology

Kimber Bogard used qualitative methods to understand the differences in reading and math performances of PreK–3 students in three schools: a top, a middle, and a low performing urban school.[3] Kimber measured many educational variables hypothesized to affect reading and math scores, such as class size, student–teacher ratios, educational and emotional climate, and teachers' years of education and training. Her results were non-significant across the board, but interestingly, "school" turned out to be a moderator of the relationships between numerous variables. For instance, in the lowest performing school, teachers' years of education were positively correlated with instructional climate and student test scores, whereas in the other two schools, no significant correlation was found. Contrary to the prediction, performance was positively correlated with class size and negatively correlated with the number of adults in class! Kimber used the pragmatic case study method developed by Dan Fishman (1999) and phenomenological analysis (Giorgi, 2009) to conceptualize many hours of interviews with teachers and administrators in all three of her schools. She found distinctive holistic structures in the three schools that enabled her to conceptualize and understand her quantitative results. She characterized the lowest performing school as "Teaching in Silos": Teachers used their own individual resources without any centralized leadership or collaborative organization. The middle achieving school structure, "Uni-directionally Coached Teaching," was organized by a gifted literary coach chosen by the principal who provided an expert model for consistent curricula, standards, and assessment tools within and across grades. In the highest scoring school structure, called "Dynamic Collective Improvisation," a visionary principal led regular, creative collaboration among teachers within and across grades who worked synergistically with each other and parents to develop integrated curricula and solve problems. These three holistic school-structures revealed how the study's variables had different meanings across the schools. All teachers agreed that their education did not well equip them for the real world of urban education, but teachers in the "Silos" school gratefully used tools from their education as best they could, explaining the positive correlation of years of education and specialized training with student performance in their school. In the "Coached" and "Dynamic Collective Improvisation" schools, teachers discarded the tools from their prior education, using, respectively, their on site expert coaching and collaborative creativity, explaining the lack of correlation between teacher education/ training and student performance. Kimber's research showed how schools vary holistically according to qualitatively determinable organizational structures. Although class sizes were greater, extra adults in classrooms were not needed in the higher performing schools because of the effective educational processes teachers implemented, whereas the teachers in the "Silos" school required lower numbers of students and additional adults to keep classroom order. Qualitative analysis of the holistic "school" variable in connection with the meanings, values, and purposes of educational variables provided empirically grounded interpretations of otherwise anomalous quantitative relationships between the educational variables and test performance.

Using Qualitative Methods to Develop a Mathematical Model: Adjustment to Graduate School

Arnond Sakworawich became interested in mathematical modeling and the perplexing problem of how one develops a mathematical model of psychological processes. He found historical cases in which such models were developed using pure logic and mathematics, whereas two psychologists who used empirical data where awarded the Nobel Prize (in Economics), Herbart Simon (1977) and Daniel Kahneman (2003). Both psychologists based their models on first and second person descriptions of cognitive processes, problem solving, and wagering, respectively, but neither reported how they derived models from qualitative data. Arnond used recently established qualitative methods to construct an ecologically valid, person-centered, mathematical model that would faithfully reflect students' adjustment to graduate school (Sakworawich, 2011). He collected 14 narrative descriptions and conducted follow-up interviews with students at various points in their graduate work. Using a creative combination of phenomenological (Giorgi, 2009; Wertz, 2010) and grounded theory (Glaser & Strauss, 1967) methods of analysis, he developed a conceptualization of the essential psychological structure and categorical variables in adjustment to graduate school. His hierarchical model of motivation, with three levels of abstraction, featured the discrepancy between present unhappiness and future goal satisfaction, including mediating variables and the context of graduate school. He used the grounded theory analytic technique of axial coding to convert mid-level general motivations into variables whose quantitative relations would represent the process of achieving happiness. Constrained and guided by the phenomenological procedure of grasping invariance through imaginative free variation, he created a mathematical equation comprehensively representing adjustment. By modeling adjustment as "happiness" (the reduction of frustration, alienation, and suffering by bringing educational achievement into line with their future goals), this model articulated variables including situational efficacy, social support, and mental toughness in terms of their meaning, value, and purpose for the student. This model specified the ways in which students can employ agency to freely transform unhappiness into happiness by clarifying ambiguities, forming new meanings, reframing interpretations, changing their values and priorities, and altering interpersonal relations and work habits to reduce the discrepancy between their actual and desired state of affairs. The mathematical model was intended for uses in graduate orientation, program evaluation, counseling, faculty-training workshops, and the development of interventions in educational institutions.

***

The rise of mixed methods research, as a new scientific standard, requires understanding the goals, limits, uses, and interrelations of qualitative and quantitative methods in psychological science. Qualitative research, independent of quantitative questions and concerns, is a necessary fundament of scientific knowledge. Empirical quantification requires qualitative knowledge as a basis of measurement and in the interpretation of numerical findings. Psychology is overcoming its problematic naiveté about qualitative research methods and methodology by clarifying the distinct yet interrelated goals of qualitative and quantitative knowledge. Detailed examination of psychological studies conducted before the term *mixed methods* emerged offer insight into how methods can be integrated. Our understanding of the fundamental importance and autonomy of qualitative methods and knowledge is changing our conception of science and our understanding of research methodology. Researchers, educators, and students formally and accountably including qualitative methods and integrating them with quantitative methods are achieving scientific goals that would otherwise elude psychology.

Notes

1. This kind of finding is not unusual. A phenomenological study of perception, which provided a descriptive knowledge of perception, concluded that little perception is included in psychological research, which in some cases does not measure perception at all (Wertz, 1983).
2. See also Wertz et al. (2017).
3. See Bogard and Wertz (2006) for a narrative of this study from the student-researcher's point of view.

References

Allport, G. W. (1942). *Use of personal documents in psychological science.* New York, NY: Social Science Research Council.

Bogard, K., & Wertz, F. J. (2006). The introduction of a qualitative perspective in advanced psychological research training: Narrative of a mixed methods doctoral dissertation. *The Humanistic Psychologist, 34*(4), 369–398.

Clampet-Lundquist, S., Edin, K., Kling, J., & Duncan, G. (2006). Moving at-risk teenagers out of high-risk neighborhoods: Why girls fare better than boys. *Princeton IRS Working Paper 509.* Princeton, NJ: Princeton University, Industrial Relations Section.

Colaizzi, P. F. (1967). An analysis of the learner's perception of the learned material at various stages of the learning process. *Review of Existential Psychology and Psychiatry, 7,* 95–105.

Colaizzi, P. F. (1973). *Reflection and research in psychology: A phenomenological study of learning.* Debuque, IA: Kendall/Hunt.

Creswell, J. W., Klassen, A. C., Piano Clark, V. L., & Clegg Smith, K. (2011). *Best practices for mixed methods research in the health sciences.* Office of Behavioral and Social Science Research, National Institutes of Health. Retrieved from http://obssr.od.nih.gov/scientific_areas/methodology/mixed_methods_research/pdf/Best_Practices_for_Mixed_Methods_Research.pdf.

Fishman, D. (1999). *The case for a pragmatic psychology.* New York, NY: New York University.

Giorgi, A. (1970). A phenomenological approach to the problem of meaning and serial learning. *Review of Existential Psychology and Psychiatry, 7,* 106–118.

Giorgi, A. (1985). *Phenomenology and psychological research.* Pittsburgh, PA: Duquesne University Press.

Giorgi, A. (2009). *The descriptive phenomenological method in psychology: A modified Husserlian approach.* Pittsburgh, PA: Duquesne University Press.

Glaser, B. G., & Strauss, A. L. (1967). *The discovery of grounded theory.* Chicago, IL: Aldine.

Gleaves, D. H., Lowe, M. R., Snow, A. C., Green, B. A., & Murphy-Eberenz, K. P. (2000). Continuity and discontinuity models of bulimia nervosa: A taxometric investigation. *Journal of Abnormal Psychology, 109*(1), 56–68.

Jahoda, M., Lazarsfeld, P. F., & Zeisel, H. (2002). *Marienthal: The sociography of an unemployed community.* New York, NY: Routledge (Originally published in 1971).

Kahneman, D. (2003). A perspective on judgment and choice: Mapping bounded rationality. *American Psychologist, 58*(9), 697–720.

Kazak, A. E. (2018). Editorial: Journal article reporting standards. *American Psychologist, 7*(1), 1–2.

Kohlberg, L. (1963). The development of children's orientation toward a moral order: Sequence in the development of moral thought. *Vita Humana, 6,* 11–33. (Reprinted in 2008, *Human Development, 51,* 8–20).

Kohlberg, L. (1971/1981). Indoctrination versus relativity in moral education. In L. Kohlberg (Ed.), *The philosophy of moral development: Moral stages and the idea of justice* (pp. 6–28). New York, NY: Harper and Row.

Kohlberg, L. (1994). *Moral development: A compendium* (Vol. 3, B. Puka, Ed.). New York: Garland Publishing (Reprint of Kohlberg, L. (1958). *The development of moral thinking and choice in the years 10 through 16.* Unpublished doctoral dissertation. Chicago, IL: University of Chicago).

Levitt, H. M., Bamberg, M., Creswell, J. W., Frost, D. M., Josselson, R., & Suárez Orozco, C. (2018). Journal article reporting standards for qualitative primary, qualitative meta-analytic, and mixed-methods research in psychology: The APA Publications and Communications Board task force report. *American Psychologist, 73*(1), 26–46.

Lilienfeld, S. O., Lynn, S. J., & Namy, L. L. (2017). *Psychology: From inquiry to understanding* (4th ed.). New York, NY: Pearson.

National Institutes of Health, Office of Behavioral and Social Sciences Research. (2001). *Qualitative methods in health research: Opportunities and considerations in application and review.* Washington, DC: Author. Retrieved from www.ssc.wisc.edu/gender/wp-content/uploads/2014/04/Qual-NIH-guidelines.pdf.

Piano Clark, V. L. (2010). The adoption and practice of mixed methods: US trends in federally funded health research. *Qualitative Inquiry, 16*(6), 428–440.

Rennie, D. L., Watson, K. D., & Monteiro, A. M. (2001). The rise of qualitative research in psychology. *Canadian Psychology, 43*(3), 179–189.

Sakworawich, A. (2011). Person-centered mathematical modeling of adjustment using phenomenological and grounded theory methods. Paper presented at *the Annual Convention of the American Psychological Association.* Washington, DC.

Simon, H. A. (1977). *Models of discovery: And other topics in the methods of science.* Dordrecht, Holland: Reidel.

Skoufalos, N. C. (2010). *The development of bulimia nervosa: A phenomenological psychological analysis* (Doctoral dissertation). New York: Fordham University. ProQuest (#3438468).

Weber, M. (1949). *Max Weber on the methodology of the social sciences* (E. A. Shils & H. A. Finch, Eds. & Trans.). Glencoe, IL: The Free Press.

Wertz, F. J. (1983). The findings and value of a descriptive approach to everyday perceptual process. *Journal of Phenomenological Psychology, 13*(2), 169–195.

Wertz, F. J. (2010). The method of eidetic analysis for psychology. In T. F. Cloonan & C. Thiboutot (Eds.), *The redirection of psychology: Essays in honor of Amedeo P. Giorgi* (pp. 261–278). Montréal, Québec: Le Cercle Interdisciplinaire de Recherches Phénoménologiques (CIRP), l'Université du Québec à Montréal et Rimouski.

Wertz, F. J. (2014). Qualitative inquiry in the history of psychology. *Qualitative Psychology, 1*, 4–16.

Wertz, F. J., Charmaz, K., McMullen, L., Josselson, R., Anderson, R., & McSpadden, E. (2011). *Five ways of doing qualitative analysis: Phenomenological psychology, grounded theory, discourse analysis, narrative research, and intuitive inquiry*. New York, NY: Guilford Press.

Wertz, F. J., Desai, M. U., Maynard, E., Morrissey, M. K., Rotter, B., & Skoufalos, N. C. (2017). Research methods for person-centered healthcare science: Fordham studies of transcendence and suffering. In M. Englander (Ed.), *Phenomenology and the social foundations of psychiatry* (pp. 95–120). London: Bloomsbury Publishing.

Yoshikawa, H., Weisner, T. S., Kalil, A., & Way, N. (2008). Mixing qualitative and quantitative research in developmental science: Uses and methodological choices. *Developmental Psychology, 44*(2), 344–354.

4 Qualitative Psychology and the New Pluralism

Kenneth J. Gergen

In the spring of 2008, Ruthellen Josselson and I addressed the governing Council of the American Psychological Association (APA) with a proposal to launch a new Division of APA. It was to be the division on Qualitative Inquiry. Although supported by a petition with over 1,000 signatures of APA members, our proposal met with stiff resistance. The most prominent critique: Qualitative inquiry is not scientific. In the end, the proposal was defeated. There remained, however, a robust wind in the sails of the qualitative enclave, and soon the Society for Qualitative Inquiry in Psychology (SQIP) was formed—outside the APA walls. Then followed long and engaging dialog with APA division heads, with the ultimate outcome that 6 years later SQIP was accepted into one of the most traditionally conservative divisions of APA. That previously named Division on Evaluation, Measurement and Statistics is now the Division on Quantitative and Qualitative Methods. At the invitation of the APA publication wing, the journal *Qualitative Psychology* was launched and now flourishes.

It would be easy enough to dismiss this dramatic turn-around as an institutional adjustment, simply appeasing the discontent of a substantial number of association members. One might also see the entry of qualitative inquiry into American psychology simply as a nod to the possibility that some observations cannot profitably be transformed into numbers. Such explanations would be blind, however, to the sweeping changes taking place across the social sciences. Traditional conceptions of knowledge, objectivity, and the place of values in our undertakings have eroded. The discipline of psychology—with deep roots in traditional conceptions—has simply been more resistant to the transformation. The qualitative movement in psychology now harbors the potential to radically transform the contours of the discipline. Most importantly, the effects of this transformation would vastly expand the contribution of the discipline to society and to the world.

In earlier work (Gergen, Josselson, & Freeman, 2015), we have discussed several of these important contributions. These include the enrichment of

theory, the inclusion of minority voices, and interdisciplinary collaboration. However, this discussion did not take sufficient account of one of the
most salient characteristics of the qualitative movement, namely its prevailing pluralism. In my view, this pluralist orientation is profound in its
transformative potential. Moreover, it adds a significant dimension to the
contribution of the movement to the profession and the world. In what follows I wish to explore the dimensions of this pluralism and underscore its
particular contributions. This will first require a brief account of the intellectual context from which the qualitative movement gained its force. Here
I will focus on the demise of foundationalist philosophy of science and
its emerging replacement. I will then center discussion on the emergent
pluralism itself. Here we can glimpse the radical range of orientations and
assumptions co-existing in the movement. As we shall see, the traditional
distinction between quantitative and qualitative research is deeply misleading. Finally, I will discuss positive contributions of this pluralism for the
future of psychology.

From Logical Positivism to Social Epistemology

Perhaps the most important contribution to the mushrooming of qualitative inquiry in the social sciences is the demise of foundational philosophy
of science and its replacement with a social epistemology. The contemporary emergence of pluralism in qualitative research may be attributed to
this same source. To briefly recapitulate, by the early twentieth century the
natural sciences had begun to bear visible fruit—harnessing power, curing
illnesses, creating weapons, and more. Philosophers took it as a challenge to
generate rational foundations for these advances. If these foundations could
be properly articulated, then it would be possible for scholars in all realms
of the academic world to become scientific and thus "productive." Drawing
from long-standing philosophic traditions, including both empiricist and
rationalist epistemologies, a variety of related accounts emerged. Within
many scientific circles, what came to be known as logical positivism served
as the received view.

It is this received view that came to serve as the rational grounds for what
many social scientists see as "mainstream science" within their respective fields. From this standpoint, the primary task of science is to generate
accurate, objective, and systematic accounts of the world. These accounts
(descriptions and explanations) are objective only insofar as they can be verified by others; their universality depends on the range of observational settings in which they are verified (or fail to be falsified). Their ultimate utility
is prediction and control. Political, ideological, and moral values are irrelevant or disruptive to establishing objective knowledge. Methods of research

should ensure that the scientist's accounts realize these ideals. Experimental methods are preferred as they warrant propositions about cause and effect. Standardized measures ensure replicability; large, representative samples lend themselves to broad generalizations; statistics add certainty to such generalizations; and a wide range of controls protect against value biases. On these grounds, qualitative research is a degraded form of inquiry; it fails on virtually all of the above criteria (See also Lamiell, this volume).

Although positivism was controversial even within philosophy itself, its grip began to deteriorate toward the end of the century. Critical analysts first began to illuminate the many ways in which seemingly neutral accounts of the world were ideologically saturated. As Michel Foucault (1978, 1980) proposed, when authoritative claims to knowledge are circulated through the society, they act as invitations to believe. Claims to knowledge function to build and sustain structures of power. A host of literary theorists and rhetoricians were simultaneously exploring the dependency of knowledge claims on the demands of language. As variously demonstrated, scientific accounts are governed by linguistic devices such as metaphor (e.g., Leary, 1994) and narrative (e.g., Gergen & Gergen, 1986).

These two lines of critique—undermining claims to value neutrality and challenging the capacity of language to map the world—set the stage for the emergence of an alternative view of science. Thomas Kuhn's *The Structure of Scientific Revolutions* (1970) is pivotal, and especially his proposal that our propositions about the world are embedded within *paradigms*, roughly a commitment to a perspective and its related methods, assumptions, and practices. Paradigms in turn are created within groups, and represent their negotiated agreements. In effect, what we take to be knowledge is lodged within socially generated perspectives. Scientific truth is only truth for those who share assumptions. This is not to denigrate empirical research, but to remove the right of any group to declare that its truths are universal. We shift from a concern with universal truth to a pragmatic vision of research accomplishments (see Slaney & Tafreshi, this volume) and the empiricist demand that a given account of the world should be accurate with respect to the way the world is. This view has been elaborated and extended by cadres of historians of science and sociologists of knowledge (e.g., Daston & Galison, 2010; Poovey, 1998). These lines of thought are often indexed as social constructionist or constructivist. By the end of the century, one could properly speak of post-foundationalism.

Qualitative Inquiry and the New Pluralism

With the shackles of foundationalist philosophy now removed, and the emerging sensitivity to multiple paradigms, the seeds of change were planted. Long suppressed minorities in psychology—psychoanalysis, phenomenology, and action researchers, among them—gained new adherents. Emerging from the postmodern debates sweeping across the sciences, new forms of inquiry—discourse analysis, narrative analysis, and hermeneutics among them—grew strong. Within neighboring disciplines in the social sciences, where foundations of science had always been shaky, creative experiments in method were burgeoning. These also began to make their way into psychology (see Schiff, this volume). Prior to the hardening of the positivist demands in psychology, there had been broader acceptance of non-experimental research—a soft pluralism. However, within the past two decades, a new pluralism has grown strong (Wertz, 2011). There is a heady sense that a new door has opened, and new horizons of inquiry are there to be explored.

Characterizing the pluralism pervading the qualitative movement is not so simple. One can gain a sense of the rainbow by simply scanning a range of popular research orientations. Included among the most visible are:

Action Research	Grounded Theory
Arts-Based Research	Hermeneutic Analysis
Auto-ethnography	Interviews
Case study	Life History
Collaborative Research	Narrative Analysis
Conversation Analysis	Participant Observation
Discourse Analysis	Phenomenology
Ethnography	Portraiture
Focus Groups	Self-Observation

This is, of course, a practice-based approach to pluralism. It emphasizes the vast range of research methods practiced within the qualitative movement. It makes evident the porous boundaries of what may be said to constitute the qualitative movement itself. Within the above listing are included practices of a century's duration along with those entering the scene within the past decade; some practices are theoretically focused in their aims, and others used in furthering corporate aims; some are chiefly concerned with social change, while others attempt to illuminate existing conditions; some have emerged in psychology and others borrowed from other disciplines. There is also continuous hybridization. For example, auto-ethnographic research represents a variation on ethnography, but arts-based researchers have borrowed from auto-ethnography to create performative auto-ethnography. The creative potentials are without clear limits.

How are we then to conceptualize the schools of thought that make up the qualitative movement? The first apparent conclusion is that the traditional distinction between quantitative and qualitative research is (and possibly always was) misleading if not obfuscating. For one, qualitative researchers can differ dramatically in the assumptions undergirding their work. To lump them, as if they share a particular philosophy of science, is groundless. Indeed, there are many researchers in the qualitative movement who share more with positivist experimentalists than with other qualitative researchers. (For example, many qualitative researchers agree with positivists in their claim to value neutrality, where others in the qualitative camp specifically reject such claims.) Nor can one separate qualitative from quantitative research on the simple grounds that one employs numerical differentiation and the other does not. (Interviews are typically viewed as qualitative, but frequency counts are often used as tools of analysis.) And too, whether a method of research is, or is not, empirical depends on how the researchers understand the method they are employing. For example, if we presume that psychological states are objective realities, then the difference between many quantitative and qualitative researchers is simply in terms of the most adequate method of representation.

In my view, we can a more usefully understand the emerging pluralism by shifting the focus from practices to the varied assumptions underlying these practices. What are the guiding assumptions that legitimize the research practices for their participants? What are the important conceptual suppositions? One might attempt to locate each method with a particular philosophy of science—logical positivism, postpositivism, and social constructionism among them. However, it would be exceedingly difficult in this case to sort the above practices in terms of philosophic school. Some of the practices have emerged within practical settings, without regard to philosophic assumptions. Others have shifted philosophic assumptions over the years. The shift in phenomenological method from a Husserlian to a Heidegerrian base, and the transformation of grounded theory from an empiricist to a constructionist metatheory are illustrative. As an alternative to identifying schools from which practices might seem to allied, it is more useful to single out conceptual lines of demarcation of traditional concern to social science inquiry. This will allow appreciation of the vast range of inquiry now arrayed under the qualitative banner.

Ontological Premises

Perhaps the chief question that may be asked of researchers is what they presume about the nature of the reality to which their research is addressed. As Danziger (1990) has demonstrated, there is a close association between one's methods of research and the associated concept of the person. There are many distinctions to be drawn here, but two overarching differences are paramount. First, a major dividing line can be drawn between researchers presuming a dualist view of human behavior as opposed to a monist. The former, and more common in qualitative inquiry, assume the existence of an inner or subjective world of experience, intentions, emotion, meaning and the like. Monists, in contrast, either disregard or abandon "mental" reality, and focus their attention on the actions of persons. Thus, for example, in narrative research, a dualist would be concerned with the capacity of an individual's story to reflect or give expression to his or her experience. For the discourse analyst, on the other hand, this dualist concern with an inner world might be replaced by an interest in the function of a given kind of narrative in social interaction or cultural life more generally. Nor do dualists themselves agree on the nature of mental process that is being expressed in one's actions. For example, while many researchers employ interviews to access the opinions, attitudes, values or intentions of the interviewees (all presumed to be accessible to the conscious mind), more psychoanalytically informed interviewers will bracket these concerns with such "superficial" content in search of repressed or unconscious motivation or desire.

A further distinction can be drawn between realists and social constructionists. For the former, the subject matter of inquiry whether personal experience, cognitive categories (on the mental side), or aggression, conversation, or social action (on the side of observable action) has palpable existence in the world. For constructionists, such essentialism is replaced by a concern with the ways in which language creates our understandings of the world. Thus, reality posits are not reflections of the world as it is, but entries into cultural life (for good or ill). It is difficult to discern the orientation of the researcher in this regard, as researchers with a constructionist orientation will make realist claims, understanding full well that the claims are socially contingent and negotiable, and have validity only for those who share traditions of understanding. In general, however, researchers focusing on discourse, conversation, or narrative will tend toward a constructionist orientation. This is owing to their understanding that assumptions about reality have their origins in language.

Epistemological Assumptions

Ontology and epistemology are closely intertwined. However, in the latter case, the focus is on assumptions about the acquisition of knowledge. We shift from what there is to know to how do we know. Most qualitative researchers share a dualist epistemology with their quantitative counterparts. That is, both presume a subject/object dichotomy, with the researcher attempting to report on the state of an independent world. However, major variations then emerge in terms of what is to be reported on and how it is to be known. We have already touched on the dichotomy between research focused on what is viewed as "publicly observed" behavior in contrast to a "mental world." It is the psychological world that most qualitative researchers place their interest. Yet, it is precisely here that we find wide variations in epistemological assumptions, that is, how can we know "the mind of the other?" Positivists have opted for rational inference, that is, attempting to use multiple methods and measures to triangulate. The early accounts of grounded theory methodology were consistent with this view. More popular within many contemporary circles is to rest conclusions—however tentative—on a process of interpretation. Yet, what is meant by interpretation is also varied. Hermeneuticists drawing from a Gadamerian or textual tradition view interpretation as a circular process of tacking back and forth between conjectures and the particulars of the individual's expression. Phenomenologists from a Hussurlian orientation might train subjects in phenomenological reporting and then search for the structure of the reports. And many narrative analysts simply treat the individual's utterances as direct expressions of his or her subjectivity. For those strongly influenced by the shift toward social epistemology, all of these many variations can be viewed as epistemological practices, realizing the socially contingent character of all epistemic assumptions.

Value Orientation

All practices of inquiry carry with them values, either implicit in the activities or located in their outcomes. The values may be embraced by the researchers who employ a given practice, they may be unconscious, or they may be inferred by others. Thus, for example, those employing experimental methods may embrace the value of value-neutral prediction. Implicitly, however, they are lending themselves to the value of an ordering of the society. Simultaneously, critics may fault the methodology for its power relations, subject-object alienation, and manipulation. In the same way there is enormous variation in the ontological premises across the spectrum of the qualitative movement, so is the pallet of values—articulated, implicit, or inferred—multihued. As many now propose, one cannot separate the pragmatic value of research from its moral, political, and ideological consequences for society (see also Slaney & Tafreshi, this volume).

This expansion in values is not simply the result of the pluralist spectrum of research practices. Rather, with the demise of positivist foundationalism, the presumption of value-neutral research also waned. As a result, in contrast to the positivist suppression of the values implicit in their research, many qualitative researchers take up a given method precisely for purposes of bettering society in their terms. Many narrative researchers, for example are deeply sympathetic to the condition of those whose narratives they share. They hope to bring collective attention, for example, to the condition of prisoners, people classified as mentally ill, immigrants, and other marginalized peoples. Critical discourse analysts will use their research to illuminate prejudices implicit in common language use, or the incoherence of a problematic political party. Participatory action research gained its very prominence in its efforts to achieve social justice.

In sum, there are no overarching ontological agreements, epistemological assumptions, set of values, or conception of research goals that unite the various endeavors now constituting the qualitative movement in psychology. Rather, we find multiplicities in each case and an open door to hybrids and new creations. In the past, researchers were generally confronted with a fixed and narrow set of scientifically acceptable methods. The challenge was to shoe-horn one's conceptual or empirical concerns into one of the sanctioned options. With the qualitative explosion, researchers may now ask themselves, "What kind of practice will best allow us to achieve our ends?" If there is no obvious "method" available for the purposes, one is free to create.

It is of special importance that in the context of the new pluralism, there is a marked absence of attempts to elevate any given orientation over the other, or to undermine or disqualify the alternatives. There appears to be an abiding recognition that there are multiple perspectives in play, and there is no means of valorizing one over another, save through selecting one perspective among many. Illustrative of this live and let live orientation is the Wertz et al. (2011) volume featuring five qualitative orientations to a single case. The contributors each demonstrate the potentials inherent in their research practice, but with no attempt to compete or diminish the alternatives. In a further sign of pluralist affinity, the subject of their collective research was also invited to join the dialog.

The Potentials of Pluralism

For the better part of the past century, psychological research has been tied to a vision of science in which the chief goal of research is to enhance prediction and control. The extent to which such an orientation has contributed to society is a subject of continuous debate. Testing abstract hypotheses is problematic, as there are no means of deriving from the abstract formulations predictions useful in any particular or unique case. A thousand experiments on dissonance reduction, for example, tell us little or nothing about people's behavior in any particular setting. Further, behavior patterns undergo continuous change, with digital technology continuously increasing the rate of change. If there were useful predictions of behavior today, they might be grossly misleading in terms of the challenges of tomorrow. As these debates continue, the new pluralism brings with it new goals of inquiry. The potentials of psychological research are resultantly expanded. Here I touch on three significant alternatives emerging from the qualitative movement.

Expanding Dimensions of Understanding

The positivist orientation to research is ideally designed to yield a single answer to questions it confronts. Because one presumes that nature is singular in its composition (we are not dealing with multiple realities), there are single, best answers as to its character. As Popper (1968) reasoned, we move closer to the truth about nature as research discards those accounts that fail to describe and predict. At the same time, in psychology, one can scarcely locate any hypotheses that have been satisfactorily discarded in this way. And too, from the standpoint of a social epistemology, singular accounts are viewed with suspicion. What nature is does not demand any (or any one) account of its nature. As we increase the range of understandings, our attention is directed in different ways; we see potentials not available before; we are alerted to outcomes otherwise suppressed.

Thus, as we expand the range of research practices, the dimensions of understanding are enriched. If we were concerned with poverty, an empirically driven study of the brain mechanisms particular to impoverished persons would be severely limited. Narrative research would vastly expand our understanding of their everyday lives. A network analysis could illuminate possible support clusters; participant observation could provide insider's insights into daily life details; action researchers could support initiatives for change and thus teach us about what can be done; and survey research might provide an indicator of the modal concerns, fears, needs, and hopes.

Opening Options for Action

It is but a short leap from understanding to action. As our frames of understanding increase, so do we locate new possibilities for action—for support, intervention, social change, policy formation, and so on. With a single answer to research about the poor, for example, we are left with but a handful of possible actions. If neurological research suggested that the brain area for hope was rarely stimulated, we might draw the conclusion that the poor were simply hard wired for this way of life, or that brain stimulation efforts would be required. Narrative researchers might elicit the kind of social concern that stimulates support programs; when support clusters are illuminated, social workers might be moved to devote special attention to collaborative efforts. The participant observer could point to small details, such as the lack of heat, light, and electricity. The results of survey researchers might be interesting to policymakers in directing attention to specific issues in employment, drugs, or schools. Action researchers could teach us from their efforts how community organizing might change the situation. And focus groups could help to expand the imagination on what may be done.

Stimulating Ethical Reflection

Positivist foundationalism is often viewed as a child of cultural modernism more generally. Central to this Zeitgeist was an attempt to bring about a productive and satisfying social order though reason and observation. Cultural modernism thus resists religious, spiritual, and philosophic movements committed to any tradition of values. Value commitments are, for the positivist, "subjective." And as reasoned, there is no means of deriving "oughts" from the careful analysis and observation of what is the case. Value-based actions should be abandoned in favor of scientific analysis, as major world conflicts are triggered by value differences. In effect, for positivists there was (and is) a pervasive resistance to value assertions and dialogs on the good.

Yet, as many critics have argued, cultural modernism has left the culture bereft of resources for ethical deliberation. As one might say of positivist foundationalism, "ethically speaking, anything goes." As described, the qualitative movement brings with it a re-invigoration of values. Vibrant enclaves within psychology now unabashedly represent, for example, feminist, LGBTQ, environmentalist, Latino, indigenous, African American, humanist, socialist, anti-psychiatry, and anti-colonialist standpoints. Ushered into presence by the movement is an invaluable sensitivity to the ethical/ideological dimensions of research. Reflection on research moves beyond the traditional confinement to methods and results to the ethical and political consequences. This respect for value-based reflection carries over, as well, into the classroom.

These three potentials—for expanding the dimensions of understanding, increasing options for action, and stimulating ethical reflection—scarcely exhaust the contribution of the new pluralism to both psychology and its publics. One might also point to the ways in which many forms of inquiry— especially in the arts-based and narrative domains—speak to non-professional audiences in ways never before available. As well, with its abandonment of the positivist efforts to fortify abstract laws, qualitative researchers direct their attention to important areas of societal concern. Not only is there a greater contribution to society, but the relationship of the discipline to society also shifts from academic isolation to dialog. There are many reasons to hope that the new pluralism signifies a major transformation of the discipline.

References

Danziger, K. (1990). *Constructing the subject: Historical origins of psychological research*. Cambridge: Cambridge University Press.

Daston, L. J., & Galison, P. (2010). *Objectivity*. Cambridge, MA: MIT Press.

Foucault, M. (1978). *The history of sexuality* (Vol. 1). New York, NY: Pantheon.

Foucault, M. (1980). *Power/knowledge*. New York, NY: Pantheon.

Gergen, K. J., & Gergen, M. (1986). Narrative form and the construction of psychological science. In T. R. Sarbin (Ed.), *Narrative psychology: The storied nature of human conduct* (pp. 22–44). New York, NY: Praeger.

Gergen, K. J., Josselson, R., & Freeman, M. (2015). The promises of qualitative inquiry. *American Psychologist, 70*(1), 1–9.

Kuhn, T. (1970). *The structure of scientific revolutions* (2nd ed.). Chicago, IL: University of Chicago Press (First published in 1962).

Leary, D. (1994). *Metaphors in the history of psychology*. Cambridge: Cambridge University Press.

Poovey, M. (1998). *A history of the modern fact: Problems of knowledge in the sciences of wealth and society*. Chicago, IL: University of Chicago Press.

Popper, K. R. (1968). *The logic of scientific discovery*. London: Hutchinson.

Wertz, F. J. (2011). The qualitative revolution in psychology. *The Humanistic Psychologist, 39*, 77–104.

Wertz, F. J., Charmaz, K., McMullen, L. M., Josselson, R., Anderson, R., & McSpadden, M. (2011). *Five ways of doing qualitative analysis: Phenomenological psychology, grounded theory, discourse analysis, narrative research, and intuitive inquiry*. New York, NY: Guilford.

5 Qualitative Methods Enhance Our Understanding and Treatment of People With Alzheimer's Disease

Steven R. Sabat

For most of the twentieth century, a biomedical approach dominated our understanding of Alzheimer's disease (AD) and attention was, therefore, focused principally on the deficits caused by the disease and the pathophysiology of the disease. Accordingly, particular cognitive functions were operationally defined and measured by using standard neuropsychological tests so as to quantify the diagnosed person's level of function in areas of memory, language, attention, calculation, executive functioning, and the like. More specifically, such tests attempting to measure these particular cognitive abilities are narrowly defined, removed from the larger social contexts in which they normally occur, and measured in isolation from one another. For example, there are separate tests for attention and for different functional aspects of language (naming objects and body parts, spelling, repeating spoken words and phrases, reading words and phrases such as in the Boston Diagnostic Aphasia Examination), and of aspects of explicit memory such as recall. In the everyday social world, attention, memory, and language (spoken conversational language, most often) do not occur in isolation from one another, but simultaneously: We pay attention to the speech of those with whom we are conversing as well as to what we, ourselves, are saying, and we retrieve the words we wish to use from long-term memory while keeping what our interlocutor is saying in working (short term) memory. Therefore, the way cognitive abilities are assayed via standard tests is quite different from the way those same cognitive abilities are deployed in typical interpersonal social life. Although these purportedly objective, quantitative, measures have been and are used in logical ways for purposes such as outcome measures in drug efficacy trials, it would be a mistake to assume that such tests are veridical measures of cognitive abilities per se in everyday life.

Problems With the Biomedical Approach

Although these measures may help us to understand what Oliver Sacks called the disease the person has, they do not enhance our understanding of what he called the person the disease has. In other words, the biomedical approach and its attendant quantitative measures do not enhance our understanding of (1) the subjective experience, the phenomenology, of AD or (2) the variety of psychological/cognitive and social abilities that can remain intact despite the progress of the disease as measured by neuropsychological tests. Ironically, it is these two areas of inquiry that are of paramount importance to the understanding and treatment of people diagnosed. One cannot provide them with optimal support without knowing their reactions to the losses they have experienced, their remaining strengths, and whether or not those psychological and social strengths are understood, respected, and engaged by their primary and secondary care partners.

Another potentially problematic aspect of the biomedical model is that seeming departures from what is considered normal behavior are frequently interpreted as being symptomatic of disease rather than as adaptations. Thus, when a person with AD says, "I went to see the, the uh, the uh . . . the person who takes care of me when I'm not well physically" instead of saying "the physician," he or she is said to be exhibiting what is considered to be a pathological behavior called, "circumlocution." It is important to note that what is being labeled as pathological here is an instance of (1) successful communication of an idea and (2) quite typical of what many otherwise healthy people do in a foreign country when they cannot think of the word for something in the local language. In such situations, we describe the characteristics, purpose, or function of the object in question and are not viewed as being pathological in the process. Instead, we are seen as adapting to the situation in the best way possible so as to communicate effectively. In the above example, although the person did not recall and speak the word physician, and although that is a deficit caused by AD, the person is not viewed and treated by evaluators as having successfully communicated. As a result, it is unfortunately and frequently the case that people diagnosed with AD are unwittingly positioned in a socially dysfunctional way (the narrative of pathology) because (1) their weaknesses are emphasized in the minds of others far more than their strengths and (2) their cognitive and social abilities in a variety of social situations are underestimated.

Such an underestimation of their strengths can lead to many forms of dysfunctional social treatment, what Kitwood called, Malignant Social Psychology (Kitwood, 1998). In other words, treatment that is depersonalizing and assaults the diagnosed person's feelings of self-worth can add greatly to the problems the person already experiences due to the brain damage caused by the disease. One form of malignant social psychology is called *labeling*, wherein the diagnosed person's actions are, if not immediately understandable by others, interpreted as symptomatic of the disease. So when Mrs. D's husband unwittingly embarrasses and humiliates her in public, and she spends the subsequent hours ignoring him, not speaking to him, Mr. D, not understanding that what he did caused his wife emotional pain, labels her righteous indignation as "irrational hostility" due to AD. In assuming that his wife's anger was due to AD, Mr. D did not see any reason to ask her why she acted in an angry manner toward him.

The Contribution of Qualitative Methods

Qualitative methods, or what A. R. Luria called, "Romantic Science" approaches, are complementary to quantitative methods. They elucidate a variety of important aspects of psychological life that are not addressed by quantitative approaches such as what the effects of Alzheimer's disease mean to the person diagnosed; the person's ability to make meaning of social situations and respond to those situations in ways that reflect lifelong dispositions; the intact aspects of selfhood; how communication between the person diagnosed and others can be enhanced despite word-finding and syntactical problems; how persons diagnosed can experience and act to avoid embarrassment and humiliation; and what caregivers can do to facilitate the use of their loved ones' remaining abilities.

During the past 25 years, a great deal of progress has been made concerning the understanding and treatment of people diagnosed with AD with regard to a number of important cognitive and social abilities. These include their subjective experience, their meaning-making ability in social situations, their ability to understand and express humor as well as a range of emotions in verbal and nonverbal terms, and the social situations that can be helpful and supportive as opposed to those that are detrimental and dysfunctional and serve to exacerbate the effects of the brain damage produced by the disease itself (see for example, Brooker, 2006; Cheston & Bender, 1999; Downs & Bowers, 2014; Harris & Caporella, 2014; Hubbard, Cook, Tester, & Downs, 2002; Hughes, 2014; Hughes, Louw, & Sabat, 2006; Kahn-Dennis, 2002; Keady et al., 2012; Killick, 2016; Kitwood, 1998; Kontos, 2004; Lokon, Kinney, & Kunkel, 2012; Moyle et al., 2016; Sabat, 1991, 2001, 2006; Snyder, 2001, 2009; Snyder, Jenkins, & Joosten, 2007). In this chapter, I will present specific examples that illustrate how the use of qualitative methods can provide information that enhances our understanding of the experience and strengths of people diagnosed and can enhance their quality of life as well as that of their care partners.

The people discussed herein were diagnosed 4 years prior to my association with them and were in the moderate to severe stages of the disease according to standard neuropsychological tests and medical examination. In each case, I developed a warm, trusting connection with the person diagnosed over a period of time that ranged between 9 months and 2 years. Their test results notwithstanding, each person could be said to be, in the words of Shweder and Sullivan (1989), a "semiotic subject." A semiotic subject is a person whose actions are driven by the meaning of the situation or circumstance in which they happen to find themselves. One can understand meaning as the following:

* Acting out of intention
* The interpretation of events and situations
* The evaluation of situations, actions, and events

Although standard neuropsychological tests were not created to reveal or measure the ability to engage in semiotic behavior, such tests can, nonetheless, reveal semiotic behavior on the part of a person diagnosed. For example, when being tested, some people diagnosed with AD will fail to answer what are, to them, relatively simple questions. Some people react by crying convulsively or becoming angry, uttering obscenities, or abruptly leaving the testing room. These reactions are labeled *catastrophic reactions* in the medical vernacular, and this term connotes pathology. One could, however, quite logically interpret such reactions as instances of semiotic behavior because the people in question are tremendously upset and perhaps angry and/or embarrassed by their failure to answer what they, themselves, judged to be simple questions that they could have answered easily at other times in their lives. In the process, they recognized their performance, evaluated its meaning as being negative to an upsetting degree, and responded in an appropriate way given the circumstances. On the other hand, if such persons did not outwardly acknowledge their errors, this behavior could be interpreted as signaling that the persons were "unaware of their deficits." So if a person with AD could act as a semiotic subject in connection with his or her performance on neuropsychological tests, could that person act as a semiotic subject in more typical, natural, social situations?

Let us address each of these aspects of meaning and explore, using narrative methods (Schiff, this volume), how a person diagnosed with AD in the moderate-to-severe stage can be appreciated as being a semiotic subject rather than someone whose condition can be understood fully in quantitative terms by his or her scores on standard tests.

Acting Out of Intention

Mrs. D, a high school graduate, was raised in a show business (Vaudeville) family, and attended an Adult Day Center program 4 to 5 days per week (Sabat, 2001). At home, she was observed to be sullen and, according to her spouse who loved and cared for her, did relatively little, so that virtually all the chores around the house fell to him to do. He did not confide to her his feelings or challenges because, in his words, "She would not understand." With the cooperation of the Day Center staff, however, she co-constructed a social role for herself at the Center, "the life of the party," by bringing good cheer to other participants who were downhearted or depressed by telling lots of old jokes and leading others in sing-alongs. In addition, she brought comfort to some participants who returned to the Day Center after having been absent due to serious illness. Mrs. D was tremendously sensitive and appropriately responsive to the emotional states of others. Social Constructionists (Harré, 1991) would refer to this aspect of selfhood as one of the multiple social personae that are subsumed under the heading of Self 3, each persona is brought into being with the cooperation of at least one other person. Indeed, Mrs. D viewed her role at the Center as being her "work" and was so successful at it that the staff asked her to help welcome new participants and integrate them into the group. On each morning that she was to go to the Day Center, she was always in a hurry to get there and would tell her husband to rush because she didn't want, in her words, "to be late for work." Mr. D confided to me that he thought the AD was growing worse because his wife was becoming, in his words, "delusional about having a job," which he construed as meaning paid employment (this is an example of labeling as defined above). When I asked her, in a good-natured, warm, teasing way about her not having told me that she had a job, she was initially puzzled by my question until I mentioned that her husband reported that she would rush him in the mornings to drive her to the Day Center. At this point, she understood immediately and explained that she viewed her cheering people up and commiserating with them as, "my work, because some of them are so depressed." It is not far afield to imagine what may have happened had all this not come to light via conversation—and if, instead, her husband told her physician that she was becoming delusional about having some kind of job. Her entire set of meaning-driven actions could have been easily construed as pathological and reflecting a worsening disease process. In fact, her sense of having "work" to do in the service of others at the Day Center was entirely consistent with being a semiotic subject—acting out of intention. She evaluated the state of others, correctly, as being sad and vulnerable and she acted intentionally in a variety of ways to lift their spirits.

In addition to attending the Adult Day Center, Mrs. D volunteered to be a subject in drug studies conducted by the NIH. When I asked her why she did that, she said that if she could do something to "help my fellow man," she was happy to do so. Of course, this meant that she subjected herself to many hours of neuropsychological tests that inevitably would reveal her inability to answer questions many of which she could easily have answered correctly in years past. Her willingness to submit to such tests was closely connected to her not having placed an overarching value on her intellectual acumen throughout her adult life. Indeed, when she experienced word-finding problems, she would often shrug them off, as it were, saying, in the style of a standup comedienne with a smile on her face, "It's that Alcazheimer's again . . . it's a helluva disease!"

Dr. M, on the other hand, a retired university professor, refused to volunteer in the same types of studies as Mrs. D. Dr. M found it tremendously aversive to be shown that she was unable to answer questions that she would have been able to answer easily in years past. She avoided such testing situations assiduously, feeling them to be assaults on her self-worth. So both women, at similar levels of severity of AD, had entirely different reactions to the same situation based on the meaning of the situation to them. Each valued their intellectual attributes in very different ways, with Dr. M valuing them very highly and Mrs. D not doing so to such an extent.

Another example of acting out of intention is seen in Mrs. K, who had severe word-finding problems and, as a result, rarely spoke. Still, she attended the Day Center 5 days per week, and it was common for her to seek out ways to help others. For example, she would frequently notice one or another participant in a wheel chair sitting in front of a closed door leading to the hallway. She would approach that person and, by gesturing, determine that the person wanted to go out of the room and offer to open the door to allow the person to exit. Mrs. K enjoyed being involved in a number of activities at the Day Center, but always avoided the small-group discussions. When discussion groups were beginning, she would either leave the room and go for a walk in the hallway or sit in another area of the Center and look through the magazines that were available for the participants. In these ways, she acted out of intention to avoid situations that were potentially embarrassing to her. Dr. M also had severe word-finding problems and reacted in a similar way to the idea of going to her support group meetings especially given that the leaders, at one time, would literally call on people in the group to provide their thoughts or reactions to something being discussed.

The Interpretation of Events and Situations

I should note here that in the above examples of acting out of intention, both women must have interpreted the meaning of the situations in question in advance of acting out of intention. In addition, their working memory and attention systems must have been functioning quite well in order for them to have evaluated the situations in question, and the prefrontal areas of their brains must have been functioning in order for them to carry out their intentions as planned (Milner, 1995; Fuster, 1995).

Dr. B, a retired university professor, attended the Day Center 2 to 3 days per week. He did not participate in any of the customary activities, clearly differentiating himself from the rest of the participants. When asked what he thought of "Trivial Pursuit," one of the games included in the program of activities, he said, "It's filler." When asked what "filler" meant, he said, "something that doesn't mean anything." He often said of the programmatic activities transpiring in a particular room, "I don't necessarily need what's in that room." In his adult life, Dr. B never involved himself with such games because, as he put it, he and his wife were "very strong academic people." Thus, he acted in accordance with his interpretation of the situations he encountered at the Day Center, an interpretation that was consistent with his proclivities throughout his adult life.

The Evaluation of Situations, Actions, and Events

Dr. B preferred to be involved with me for 2 hours a day, 2 to 3 times per week, on what he called, "The Project," which was my work on elucidating the subjective experience of AD (Sabat, 2001). I explained to him and to his wife that I wanted to learn about what it's like for a person to have AD and that I needed their help toward that end. This work was, in his words, "a scientific sort of thing," and he noted that, "we can get glory from this," and that this work "gave status." He was able to evaluate the worthiness of situations and events in accordance with his lifelong academic proclivities and dispositions in spite of the fact that he was in the moderate to severe stage of AD according to objective biomedical and neuropsychological measures. In becoming my research collaborator, one of his important Self 3 personae (in Social Constructionist theory), endured as long as he received my cooperation and that of the staff. To differentiate himself further from the other participants at the Day Center, he asked the staff to post a sign in the hallway on which the work schedule for "The Project" was written: the days and times when he and I would meet to talk. In this and other ways, he sought to present himself as something more than an Adult Day Center participant diagnosed with AD. Indeed, in his view and in his own stated words, "I'm a scientist, for heaven's sake!" Although he was retired from his university position and no longer engaged in any scientific work consistent with his decades-long academic vocation, his habits of mind remained very much coeval with being a scientist, and he evaluated the worthiness and value of situations from that point of view.

Mrs. D provides another example of the evaluation of situations by a person with AD in the moderate to severe stages. She and her husband slept in different, but adjoining, bedrooms in their home. The bathroom on the main level of the house was closest to the bedroom in which Mr. D slept. When

Mrs. D had to use the bathroom in the middle of the night, she always used the bathroom in the basement. When I inquired as to why she used the basement bathroom instead of the more convenient one only a few steps away from her bedroom, she said, "My husband is a light sleeper." Thus, she evaluated the meaning of the situation in a way that reflected her concern for her husband's well-being—using the bathroom next to his bedroom might wake him up, and she did not want to do that. This was consonant with the attribute of being a considerate, loving wife, and partner for decades of married life.

Mrs. L was also in the moderate-to-severe stages of AD, and her husband of many decades was her primary care partner. Mr. L reported that he had engaged a nurse to help his wife bathe; he believed that she was unable to do so herself. Whenever the nurse came to their house for that purpose, according to Mr. L, Mrs. L cried convulsively. This was not something that she did routinely in their daily lives, save for this situation. I asked Mr. L if his wife had always been a rather modest person when it came to personal hygiene and if she believed it to be something that was very private. He replied that she always was modest in that regard and that she did believe that bathing and the like belonged in a very private domain. This was the case, he said, for their decades-long marriage. It was not her custom to be seen unclothed, especially by a stranger, and so this situation was terribly embarrassing and, perhaps, saddening and humiliating to Mrs. L. Seemingly, she was out of control of something that was so utterly personal and private to her. She thus evaluated the meaning of this situation and acted as a semiotic subject. Herein, we see how the context of the situation (Schiff, this volume) and its meaning were of paramount importance.

There are no standard neuropsychological tests or other medical means of evaluating people with AD that would have revealed or predicted the semiotic behavior exemplified in these people's actions and words. This is especially important to understand because such actions reveal cognitive and social strengths that are as admirable as they are important and that seem to survive the brain injury that results from the moderate to severe stage of AD. Therefore, (1) qualitative methods are able to reveal these aspects of the phenomenology of AD and the social strengths that persist; (2) quantitative methods cannot do so; and (3) the two approaches are quite different from one another in terms of what they can reveal about the person diagnosed.

Is the Qualitative Approach Valid?

If validity means the degree to which a method of investigation does what it purports to do, then, the answer is yes. The qualitative method exemplified by the above narratives reflects the attempt to understand what Sacks called, "the person the disease has" and succeeds in doing so in ways that quantitative approaches have not and, indeed, cannot. This is true for a number of reasons.

First, qualitative methods reveal the nuanced, dynamic nature of the phenomenology of AD because they can capture the variety of personal histories, values, social lives, and meaning-making ability of the people diagnosed. In a sense, the narratives parallel Yamina's (Schiff, this volume) in that a nuanced understanding of each person's meanings can be appreciated. These important attributes of individual people cannot be captured by numerals. That is to say, they cannot be "measured" (see Lamiell, this volume). Nonetheless, they are crucially important because the way a person experiences AD is connected intimately to his or her values, the meaning that the person places on the dysfunctions caused by AD, and the ways he or she is treated by others. For example, we appreciate this clearly in the remarkably different ways that Mrs. D and Dr. M responded to their word-finding problems and to the prospect of volunteering for drug studies to name but two examples.

Second, qualitative methods do not seek from the outset to discern abstract general laws (meaning "true on average"—see Lamiell, this volume), about the lived experience of AD but seek instead primarily to preserve and convey the lived reality of each person involved. This can be seen as conforming to the spirit of Stern's (1938) point of view about the virtue of studying individuals rather than variables (see Lamiell, this volume). It is this lived reality, after all, that is important to understand if the goal is to help individuals diagnosed and their care partners to cope as best they can with the intrusion of the disease and its effects into everyone's life. This is precisely the opposite of arriving at some depersonalized average value in what is all too often a vain attempt to discern a general, or universal, law. If there are any commonalities that exist in connection with the phenomenology of AD, they will be found by looking at the information gleaned from many individuals over the course of time. The initial goal then, is not to unearth a general law (or, even less desirable, an average value). If patterns emerge from the qualitative studies of people with AD, they can appreciated as such, and we can begin to theorize about commonalities in their experiences. Indeed, qualitative methods have led to "person-centered" approaches to helping people with AD (Brooker, 2006; Downs & Bowers, 2014) rather than "one size fits all" approaches that are seen with contemporary drug interventions.

Third, a criticism that has been leveled against this approach is that it's "only telling stories" (de Medeiros, 2013, personal communication)—implying that the qualitative approach, as exemplified by the narratives presented above, is itself less valid than what is learned from randomized controlled trials involving the analysis of group data via inferential statistics. What those who argue this line of thinking seemingly fail to recognize is that the journal articles containing quantitative analyses of test performances by a group of people diagnosed with AD as compared with a group of healthy control subjects, for example, are also "telling stories," albeit stories of a very different type. The stories that I uncovered, missing in the experimental literature, display semiotic subjects and the intact selfhood by people with AD. These stories are about people and their remaining psychological strengths despite their diagnoses. However, the stories of statistically significant differences between groups of people diagnosed and those deemed healthy on tests or on tasks presented in an experimentally oriented laboratory or hospital clinic are not about any individual person at all. Rather, they are about particular cognitive processes such as memory or attention or this or that aspect of language function, to name but a few, or about the effects of a drug on those processes. Indeed, such stories convey information about the cognitive processes of a mythical average individual with AD compared with those of a mythical average healthy person, or of a mythical average person with AD taking an experimental drug compared with a mythical average person with AD taking a placebo. Ironically, to engage in semiotic behavior of the type I have discussed, a person must possess intact cognitive abilities such as attention and executive function of the kind that is required to assess a situation and possible outcomes from different actions—hypothetical thinking and social cognition, to name a few.

Is the Qualitative Approach Scientific?

Harré (2004) provides a refreshing analysis regarding this question. He argues that the human and natural sciences are fundamentally different in terms of the phenomena they seek to study. The phenomena of the human sciences are meaningful in that the human sciences study the "intentional properties of things and events," whereas the natural sciences study phenomena "with respect to their material properties" (Harré, 2004, p. 5). One example he provides may serve to bring the intentional and the material aspects of a phenomenon into sharp focus: A sound has material properties such as loudness (in decibels) and pitch (in frequency), and these properties are in the domain of natural sciences. If, however, that sound comes to have a role in human life, as a warning for instance, it takes on "intentional properties" and falls into the realm of human science, such as psychology (Harré, 2004, p. 5). To the extent that qualitative methods deal with intentionality in human discourse—what people say and do—they are particularly appropriate for human sciences. To be more specific, he proposes, "Psychology is the scientific study of meaning making and management and the skills necessary to accomplish it" (2004, p. 4). He posits further that the material aspects of human life are surely open to quantitative analysis, where quantitative is understood to be mathematical rather than statistical. The intentional aspects of human life, however, are not open to this kind of analysis: "We have no idea how semantic, intentional properties of phenomena could be quantified. Neither Likert scales nor statistical analyses of populations of cases make any sense in the domain of meanings" (Harré, 2004, p. 6).

In connection with Likert scales, we can appreciate yet another irony. If a person were to say, "I feel very cold in here," that testimony is often dismissed as being "merely subjective" or "anecdotal." Interestingly, we never hear anyone say that a piece of information is "merely objective." If, however, one were to give that same person a Likert scale and a pencil and there were a statement such as "I feel very cold in here" at the top and beneath the statement were five bubbles in which the person is instructed to make a mark with the pencil, something different happens. The person marks the bubble next to "strongly agree" (as opposed to "mildly agree," "neutral," "mildly disagree," and "strongly disagree"), and now, magically, we have "real data." Clearly, this is not the kind of quantitative analysis to which Harré refers and sees as being fruitful in the human sciences. If we shifted the topic from whether or not a person found meaning or made meaning in a particular social situation, this kind of analysis would tell us only "that" the person did or did not, but would not begin to address the question of "why" the person did or did not; that is, what was the meaning involved and what exactly did the person say and do? It seems to me that "that" and "why" are very different, but complementary, ways of understanding. The area of human sciences, that of intentionality, requires a level of analysis other than the numerical, proposes. Toward that end Harré, directs our attention to the contributions of Wittgenstein (1952), and extensions therefrom, regarding the role of language.

Therefore, whether one engages in qualitative or quantitative research, the reports of that work are, themselves, stories or narratives, and it behooves us as academics, as scientists, who seek the truth to admit to that reality. In so doing, it may be simultaneously possible for investigators of all orientations to appreciate A. R. Luria's idea that these different methods are indeed complementary to one another and that neither one alone can lay claim to being the one and only path to discovering all that is true about people. Depending on what it is one wants to know, one or another method is preferable. Adopting a pragmatic tool-based approach with regard to methods employed (see Slaney & Tafreshi, this volume) is of great value.

If one wants to understand the dynamic nature of the subjective experience, the phenomenology, of people diagnosed with AD, their meaning-making ability, and their psychosocial strengths, one needs to employ qualitative methods that give pride of place to the discourse of such people: what they say and do in the natural social world—the world that is not represented in any laboratory manipulation or hospital clinic. To deny the value of their voices and the important strengths that their actions in the everyday social world reveal ignores a source of tremendously valuable knowledge. In addition, it is a species of disrespectful marginalization that is unbecoming to those who purport to value human life in all its diverse expressions and who seek to improve the quality of life of people diagnosed. Christine Bryden (2015), diagnosed with early onset dementia though not of the Alzheimer's type, has authored a number of books and spoken at international conferences frequently since that diagnosis. She has strongly suggested, regarding the research efforts focused on dementia, that there should be "nothing about us without us." I heartily agree and urge that we consider the importance of this message seriously, for the quality of life of millions of people diagnosed as well as their care partners hangs in the balance.

References

Brooker, D. (2006). *Person-centred dementia care: Making services better*. London: Jessica Kingsley Publications.

Bryden, C. (2015). *Nothing about us without us*. London: Jessica Kingsley Publications.

Cheston, R., & Bender, M. (1999). *Understanding dementia: The man with the worried eyes*. London: Jessica Kingsley Publishers.

Downs, M., & Bowers, B. (2014). *Excellence in dementia care: Research into practice* (2nd ed.). New York, NY: McGraw Hill Education.

Fuster, J. (1995). Two temporal perspectives of frontal lobe function. In H. H. Jasper, S. Riggio, & P. S. Goldman-Rakic (Eds.), *Epilepsy and the functional anatomy of the frontal lobe*. New York, NY: Raven Press.

Harré, R. (1991). The discursive production of selves. *Theory and Psychology, 1*, 51–63.

Harré, R. (2004). Staking our claim for qualitative psychology as science. *Qualitative Research in Psychology, 1*, 3–14.

Harris, P. B., & Caporella, C. A. (2014). An intergenerational choir formed to lessen Alzheimer's disease stigma in college students and decrease the social isolation of people with Alzheimer's disease and their family members: A pilot study. *American Journal of Alzheimer's Disease and Other Dementias, 29*, 270–281.

Hubbard, G., Cook, A., Tester, S., & Downs, M. (2002). Beyond words: Older people with dementia using and interpreting nonverbal behavior. *Journal of Aging Studies, 16*, 155–167.

Hughes, J. C. (2014). *How we think about dementia*. London: Jessica Kingsley Publishers.

Hughes, J. C., Louw, S. J., & Sabat, S. R. (Eds.). (2006). *Dementia: Mind, meaning, and the person*. Oxford: Oxford University Press.

Kahn-Dennis, K. (2002). The person with dementia and artwork: Art therapy. In P. B. Harris (Ed.), *The person with Alzheimer's disease: Pathways to understanding the experience*. Baltimore, MD: The Johns Hopkins University Press.

Keady, J., Jones, L., Ward, R., Koch, S., Swarbrick, C., Hellstrom, I., . . . Williams, S. (2012). Introducing the bio-psycho-social model of dementia through a collective case study design. *Journal of Clinical Nursing, 22*, 2768–2777.

Killick, J. (2016). Creativity and dementia. In C. Clarke & E. Wolverson (Eds.), *Positive psychology approaches to dementia*. London: Jessica Kingsley Publishers.

Kitwood, T. (1998). *Dementia reconsidered: The person comes first*. Philadelphia, PA: Open University Press.

Kontos, P. (2004). Ethnographic reflections on selfhood, embodiment and Alzheimer's disease. *Ageing and Society, 24*, 829–849.

Lokon, E., Kinney, J. M., & Kunkel, S. (2012). Building bridges across age and cognitive barriers through art: College students' reflections on an intergenerational program with elders who have dementia. *Journal of Intergenerational Relationships, 10*, 337–354. doi:10.1080/15350770.2012.724318

Milner, B. (1995). Aspects of human frontal lobe function. In H. H. Jasper, S. Riggio, & P. S. Goldman-Rakic (Eds.), *Epilepsy and the functional anatomy of the frontal lobe*. New York, NY: Raven Press.

Moyle, W., Venturato, L., Cooke, M., Murfield, J., Griffiths, S., Hughes, J., & Wolf, N. (2016). Evaluating the capabilities model of dementia care: A non-randomized controlled trial exploring resident quality of life and care staff attitudes and experiences. *International Psychogeriatrics, 28*, 1091–1100.

Sabat, S. R. (1991). Facilitating conversation via indirect repair: A case study of Alzheimer's disease. *Georgetown Journal of Languages and Linguistics, 2*, 284–96.

Sabat, S. R. (2001). *The experience of Alzheimer's disease: Life through a tangled veil*. Oxford: Blackwell.

Sabat, S. R. (2006). Implicit memory and people with Alzheimer's disease: Implications for caregiving. *American Journal of Alzheimer's Disease and Other Dementias, 21*, 11–14.

Shweder, R., & Sullivan, M. (1989). The semiotic subject of cultural psychology. In L. Previn (Ed.), *Handbook of personality theory and research*. New York, NY: Guilford.

Snyder, L. (2001). The lived experience of Alzheimer's: Understanding the feelings and subjective accounts of persons with the disease. *Alzheimer's Care Quarterly, 2*, 8–22.

Snyder, L. (2009). *Speaking our minds: What it's like to have Alzheimer's* (Rev. ed.). Baltimore, MD: Health Professions Press.

Snyder, L., Jenkins, C., & Joosten, L. (2007). Effectiveness of support groups for people with mild to moderate Alzheimer's disease: An evaluative survey. *American Journal of Alzheimer's Disease and Other Dementias, 22*, 14–19.

Stern, W. (1938). *General psychology from the personalistic standpoint* (Translated from the German by H. D. Spoerl). New York, NY: The Macmillan Company (Original work published 1935).

Wittgenstein, L. (1952). *Philosophical investigations*. Oxford: Blackwell.

6 Understanding Psychology, Differently

Brian Schiff

Psychology doesn't study persons. Curiously, mainstream psychology is about something else. Abstract and quantifiable objects meant to depict psychological phenomena, and variables are the main preoccupation and product of academic psychology. Our journals are filled with variables, strategies for measuring them, descriptions of their properties, and relations to other variables. Institutionalized in the middle of the twentieth century, variable-centered research is the common metric for studying all psychological problems (Danziger, 1997; Lamiell, this volume). For the mainstream, it is the *standard practice*—the one and only way of doing psychological science.

I want to emphasize that there is nothing inherently wrong with studying variables. For certain research questions, it is the most appropriate method. The problem is that not all psychological questions, or even the most crucial ones, are answerable using variable-centered methods. Strangely enough, psychology's method of choice is not equipped to observe how psychological phenomena play out in the thoughts, experiences, and reflections of persons.

To study human psychology, the logic of variable-centered methods is, at best, circuitous and, at worse, hopelessly flawed. Researchers begin from the premise that they are interested in psychological qualities, how persons think, feel, or interpret action, but quickly move to the formulation of variables to represent how these qualities work at the individual level of analysis. Variables are then, usually, measured on individuals—persons fill out surveys or are observed. But, their responses are analyzed statistically at the level of the group.

As a description of the group, there is no logical problem. The trouble begins when researchers attempt to move from the group level, the sample, and what the sample estimates about the population, to the level of the person and their psychological experience. But, going back to the person is impossible. Researchers imbue the variables themselves with agency *as if* they exist in a psychological relationship rather than a statistical relationship and *as if* they interact with or effect each other. They don't—their relationship is merely a statistical one observed in the pattern of results across the group. But, researchers make the suspicious move of applying the findings from the group level to the individual. If the relationship exists at the level of the group, then, in some measure, it is fallaciously supposed to exist in the person (Lamiell, 2003).

I want to go one step further. Even if we know that two variables co-occur, they are correlated, and even if, looking at our raw data we know that the pattern of responses in one individual are exactly in the same direction observed at the group level of analysis, we have no basis for knowing *if* they are related on the psychological level because we have not observed it. The method of analysis did not penetrate into the connective fiber of how persons tie together thoughts and experiences that might have led to scores on this variable and that variable.

The problem is not remediable with the introduction of mediating and moderating variables or more complex methods of analysis. It is trenchant and represents the most devastating logical oversight of contemporary psychology. Rather than dealing with the workings of psychological phenomena, researchers are left with decontextualized and disembodied fragments without a good sense of how psychological relationships function in the experience of persons.

This is exactly where qualitative methods can make a substantial contribution to psychological science. Qualitative methods can, indeed, reach the psychological level and can do so in a way that is scientifically credible. In particular, I will argue that one variant of qualitative methods, narrative psychology, is a powerful tool for starting to put the pieces back together again to understand the connections that persons make interpreting their experiences. Narrative offers the rare opportunity for a more integrated view of human psychology by accounting for multiple influences and levels of analysis, simultaneously, and proposing complex models for the way that persons interpret experience, self, and world.

Although the aims of this chapter are theoretical, I want to make the above points explicit through the examination of a concrete problem. I compare research on the identities of Palestinians with Israeli citizenship from two methodological perspectives. First, I consider the limitations of quantitative research for studying identity. Next, I present a close reading of one of my research interviews as a way of demonstrating how narrative can add to scientific psychology by exploring the interpretations that persons make about their experiences.

Palestinian Citizens of Israel

There are nearly 1.5 million Palestinians with Israeli citizenship living inside the borders of Israel, representing about 20% of the population of

Israel (Central Bureau of Statistics State of Israel, 2008). Although linked by history, kinship, culture, religion, and language with the Arabs of the Levant and the Palestinians in the West Bank, Gaza, and the diaspora, the Palestinians in Israel represent a distinct social group unto themselves. They participate in most aspects of Israeli society, from the government to agriculture and, in large measure, have chosen to work within the laws of the state to accomplish their political ends.

Although they are Israeli citizens and share many of the same rights as Jews under the law, there continue to exist ethnically biased laws favoring Jews, especially in the areas of citizenship and landownership. There are also glaring differences in economic status and the distribution of public services (Pappé, 2011). State symbols and institutions are based upon Jewish nationalist principles. Indeed, there is a basic contradiction in the aspiration to be a Jewish state and democratic one when a substantial minority is not Jewish (Rouhana, 1997). The Jewish majority often views the Arab minority with suspicion, as the other, even as the enemy.

Although many Palestinians in Israel are attracted to the Palestinian nationalist narrative, other resources for understanding themselves and their place in the social world are available and, can be, viable options. There is the possibility of identifying with the State of Israel or Israeli Jewish society, which, in some quarters, can be culturally and politically progressive. Palestinians could also identify with the Arab world, including a desire for a pan-Arab state and/or culture. Globalized values and social mores are also found widely in the media and represent yet additional possibilities (Rabinowitz & Abu-Baker, 2005). This complex mix of potential identity resources can be thought of as *identity streams* (Schiff, 2002).

As early as the 1960s, social scientists have investigated how Palestinians in Israel describe their identities (Peres & Yuval-Davis, 1969). Since that time, numerous large- and small-scale research projects have surveyed Palestinian's sense of affiliation and affection for various identity labels. These variable-centered studies debate the balance between belonging to the Palestinian national group versus an Israeli civic identity. Some researchers have argued that there is a conflict in managing these identities (Hoffman & Rouhana, 1976), while others have argued for increasing affinity to the Palestinian (Rouhana, 1997) or Israeli identity (Smooha, 1999, 2005).

Variable Identities

I want to take a close look at a fairly recent study by Amara and Schnell (2004), "Identity repertoires among Arabs in Israel," to explore what a variable-centered approach to the study of a psychological problem, such as identity, misses. One should note that the logical errors in this study are endemic in the literature in psychology and not peculiar to this study or line of research.

Amara and Schnell's (2004) research is a thought provoking and well-executed investigation of the identity structures of the Arabs in Israel. There are several reasons why this study is noteworthy. First, Amara and Schnell consider identity as a multidimensional, rather than singular, phenomenon with the potential for multiple simultaneous affiliations and affections. Using the metaphor of identity repertoires, they theorize identity as a pluralistic orchestration with various arrangements. Second, the research is sensitive to the social and cultural contexts of identity. Finally, they employ a deliberate method of sampling with 500 men and women from five diverse locations across Israel, conscientiously striving for diversity in age, religion, and socio-economic status.

Each of the 500 participants rated the importance of six possible identities (Arab, Palestinian, Israeli, Religion, Clan, and Home Community) from irrelevant (0) to very important (6) and answered an open-ended question about what makes them proud or not proud of these identities. Examining the distribution, they find that the average means of Arab (4.9) and Religious identity (4.6) are rated highest, followed by Palestinian (3.1) and Israeli (2.9) with home community (1.7) and clan (1.3) marginal. They also note the wide variability demonstrated by large standard deviations.

One of the most intriguing findings is that 77% of their participants rated at least three or more identities as a 4 or higher, meaning that for most individuals, multiple identities are very salient. Amara and Schnell conduct two analyses, correlational and cluster, of the relationship between these identities.

In the correlational analysis, they note that only two correlation coefficients show values of over .4. Palestinian and Israeli identities are negatively correlated ($\sigma = -0.52$, $p < .0000$), and Clan and Community are positively correlated ($\sigma = 0.44$, $p < .0000$). Amara and Schnell consider these correlations "relatively weak," but in fact, in the psychological literature, they are strong.

In the cluster analysis, they describe five distinct clusters: (1) "Autonomous Arabs" loading on Arab, Religion, and Palestinian identities and representing 46% of the sample, (2) "Arab Israelis" loading on Arab, Religion, and Israeli identities and representing 31% of the sample, (3) "Arab Nationalists" loading on Arab and Palestinian identities and representing 14% of the sample, (4) "Druze" loading on Religion and Israeli identities and representing 5% of the sample, and (5) "Israeli Druze" loading on Israeli and Religion and representing 4% of the sample.

Although this information is interesting in a demographic sense, it provides little information about the psychology of the persons studied

(Lamiell, this volume). Variables are related in the group, they show a statistical relationship, but we know nothing about how these identities are meaningfully connected on the psychological level. For example, in the correlation analysis, the group-level statistics tell us that there is a tendency for the Palestinian and Israeli identity variables to be negatively related ($\sigma = -.52$). This means that when responding to Amara and Schnell's questions, persons in the sample tended to rate one high and the other low. But the correlation does not provide us with any information about how persons interpret these identities. Why do persons rate one high and the other low (or not)? How do they orchestrate them in their thoughts and reflections about self, life, and world? We don't have any answers to these questions because, simply, they were not studied.

The same criticism applies to the cluster analysis. Yes, in the group, these identities do appear to go together and to differentiate between different patterns of self-ratings, but we still have no idea how persons manage these identities. Why are they clustered? Tellingly, Amara and Schnell give labels to each of the clusters, such as "Autonomous Arabs" or "Arab Israelis," but these are the researchers' labels and not those of the persons involved. It is simply not true, as the researchers state, that "close to one-third of the respondents define themselves as Israeli Arabs" (p. 185). Rather, the researchers define them this way on the basis of their analysis. The person never makes the connections between the identities—it is researcher who does so. Once again, the variables are statistically related, but the psychological relationship is occluded.

To their credit, Amara and Schnell recognize the importance of meaning. "One problem that was not addressed in most identity research performed on the Arab community in Israel was the question of how people understand the meaning of each identity in the repertoire" (p. 187). I thoroughly agree. Their solution is to ask participants "to say in a few sentences what makes them feel proud or not proud of each of their identities" (p. 187). The results section ends with several quotes about each of the six identities. The quotes are interesting, but there is no indication of who said them or what they mean other than the fact that one of the participants in the study felt this way. In other words, there is no context that would make the quotes understandable about the experience of a person. Despite the attempt to address meaning, the end product remains fragmented and decontextualized.

Narrating Identity

In the variable-centered frame, there is no pathway out of this conceptual imbroglio toward meaning. But, there are viable alternatives to variable-centered approaches. As I have argued (Schiff, 2017), a narrative perspective on human lives allows researchers to bring problem and method in direct conversation with each other to make observations about how basic psychological phenomena work. By studying persons one at a time and closely listening to how they make connections between various aspects of their life experience, researchers can observe the kinds of basic psychological phenomena that Amara and Schnell are interested in but are unable to access. The only route to answering the question "How do Palestinians understand their identities?" is to focus our attention on a single person to discover how this person understands their identity in their thoughts and reflections.

Narrative research is centered on making visible and open for analysis the interpretations that persons make about self, life, and world. Although the focus is on interpretations, analysis goes beyond *what* was said and *how* it was said. Inquiry includes a consideration of the speaker's life circumstances, family and unique personality and experience (*who* is speaking), but also extends outward into aspects of time (*when*) and space (*where*) that frame every interpretation. Such questions are not an ending point, but are useful in uncovering and describing the dynamics of interpretations and developing theories of *why*.

To flesh out the complex matter of interpreting identity, we need to study a person. Therefore, I focus on a single interviewee, Yemina, one of 24 Palestinians students with Israeli citizenship at the Hebrew University of Jerusalem that I interviewed between 2012–2015. The group included students from across Israel, both women and men, Muslims and Christians. Interviews were conducted in English and designed as dialogues to investigate reflections and stories about who they are now and how they arrived at these self-understandings.

Although the social and political circumstances of Palestinians in Israel are enormously complex, for my interviewees, the tensions are acute. Like youth everywhere, they are engaged in the project of identity exploration and political discovery and must find a position in the social and political landscape of their time and place. As Arabs attending one of Israel's most prestigious institutions of higher learning, they have the potential to become integrated into Israel's intellectual and economic establishment. Finally, coming to the university presents opportunities for interacting with Israeli Jews in an unstructured environment. In Israel, primary and secondary schools are, largely, segregated. But, the Hebrew University, like other Israeli universities, is mixed. In 2008/2009, Arabs were 10% of the student population at Israeli universities (Central Bureau of Statistics State of Israel, 2008/2009).

Students recounted their identities in a variety of ways. Some spoke of a consistent and singular Palestinian identity, while others were trying to enter the Jewish social world. Although some interviewees framed identity as settled, others resisted categorization or viewed the question as a persistent and ongoing concern. As Yemina described:

> It's just too complicated. You don't really know who you belong to? Which category, because we're all categorized here. So you don't know which category you belong to. I kind of like to refrain from any category, because I don't like being categorized. I accept that I am, but I just don't like the fact that I am. So, I just live. I like showing myself as a human, rather than A, B, C . . . I'm a female. I'm an Arab. I'm an Arab-Israeli. I'm none of this. I just like accepting and taking things as a human being. I try my best.

A frequent refrain found in the interviews is a sense of fragmentary closeness and estrangement from both Palestinian and Israeli worlds in which all identities are inadequate. I conceptualize this liminal status as "non-belonging."

As will become apparent, Yemina's life is, in some ways, "atypical." But, when we begin to fix our attention on any given person, we soon realize that no life is typical. I don't intend Yemina's interview to stand in for the entire group of interviewees. But, in relation to the group, Yemina does, like about half of the interviewees, prominently give voice to a sense of non-belonging and similarly, like about half of the interviewees, the university has effected a change in her identity.

Yemina grew up, and still lives, with her Muslim family in a village near Jerusalem. They are working class; Yemina and her siblings are the first generation to attend university. When I spoke with her, she was finishing her bachelor's in the social sciences. Interestingly, the family only recently became citizens. The decision was pragmatic—to obtain passports for travel. But they were also concerned that the village might become part of an eventual Palestinian state and wanted to ensure that they wouldn't be forced out of their home.

After framing the interview as a conversation about identity, I allow some space for her to begin. Somewhat tentatively, she introduces herself "I'm Yemina. I don't know how to start." I ask, "Where are you from?" She responds, "I'm from Jerusalem. I grew up here my whole life. I was born here. I grew up in a very difficult area here."

The "difficult area" and exactly how Yemina's family and upbringing make village life so difficult is a major subject of discussion. As she says a little later:

> It's very conservative and it does not allow other religions. It's like an all Muslim village. . . . Very traditional culture. Not all of them are religious, but they try to be in a very strict way. . . . Women staying at

home, doing all these domestic . . . obligations. . . . So, I couldn't find myself fitting in this village, but I still grew up there.

Although for other interviewees non-belonging often entailed differentiating the self from the family, for Yemina, it is not a rebellion against her immediate family. The distance that she feels with her extended family and community is her parents' inheritance. Yemina's father was born in the village, but spent his childhood in Germany. She says, "So, he had this kind of Europeanized/Arabized kind of grain." Yemina's mother is from outside the village and outside of the extended family's values. The marriage has been a source of conflict for over 20 years. As she says, "even with my own grandparents (who live next door) . . . they don't really accept the way we are, the way we live." When asked what they don't accept, Yemina responds:

> The religious. The fact that both me and my sister and my mom are not with hijabs. The fact that we married late or aren't married yet. The fact that we go to a mixed school. That we speak English better than Arabic. We're not religious. . . . The fact that my mom works and she's not the typical, domestic wife. . . . Me and my parents, as in my family, still feel strangers towards my dad's side of the family.

One of the consequences of her family's values was their choice of schools. Rather than sending their children to the local school where students are required to wear a hijab in class, Yemina and her three siblings attended an international school at some distance from their home that supports her parents' liberal and international views.

One of the unforeseen results is that Yemina's English is better than her Arabic.

> The thing is, I wasn't attached to Arabic at all. I wasn't attached to Arabic religion. I wasn't attached to Arabic grammar. . . . So when I found the opportunity that I can be into another language, I just did it all the way. I started reading books in English. I've never read a book in Arabic, never. . . . I don't know Arabic authors. I don't know Arabic old singers. I don't know anything. I'm not even attached to the Arabic culture, you know. So, I just never thought that Arabic would represent me, but I'm still an Arab. So I do know about the culture, but I just can't write in Arabic. If someone would ask me to write a book or story about myself . . . I'd write it in English.

Although Yemina recounts a considerable distance with the values and lifestyle of her fellow villagers and although her emotional attachment to

Arab language and culture seems thin, it is important to note that she still maintains a connection. As I have already shown, she would prefer to avoid categorization, but somewhat reluctantly, Yemina does state:

> The thing is, I don't really think about identity. Like, I don't walk in the street thinking that I'm an Arab Palestinian. No. Palestinian–Arab–Israeli citizen. It's that complicated. So I never really think deeply about it. But if I had—I'd know that far. Like, if someone would tell me to completely erase my Palestinian–Arab thing, I wouldn't. Because then, what else would I be to others, you know? To me, I am who I am, but to people around me who are actually accepting this categorization, I would just be in an undecided category which is—I wouldn't say bad, but it's just that they would avoid your existence.

Her explanation is focused on how others understand her rather than affection, but some pull toward the identity is apparent. Although she differentiates herself from other Arabs, she would not jettison the identity altogether.

Coming to the Hebrew University of Jerusalem also plays a large role in her identity story. Yemina's path to the Hebrew University was far from direct. Her dream was to study in the United States, and she was accepted to several universities there, but despite fellowships, the expense was prohibitive. She never imagined herself studying at an Israeli university and certainly not in Hebrew. Her Hebrew language skills were non-existent. But, faced with the financial realities, her mother drove her down the street to the Hebrew University to speak with one of the admissions counselors. She found herself enrolled in basic-level Hebrew courses, learning the alphabet, and studying for a transitional degree.

Interestingly, her studies provide the motivation for contact with Israeli Jews and the opportunity to see them differently. One critical experience that she recounts is volunteering as a vote observer in the Knesset elections. She was the Joint List's (a confederation of Arab parties) representative—in the occupied territories! I ask, "What inspired you to do something like that?" Yemina answers:

> I don't like always being on the dark side. I don't like . . . not knowing what's going on. . . . This year, I actually wanted to know what would happen. I study the social sciences, so it's all about knowing. So, I really wanted to know. What would go on that day? . . . I really wanted to observe it.

Not only does the experience bolster Yemina's sense of being a legitimate part of the Israeli political system, but even representatives of the right wing parties meet her with respect. Interestingly, she enters into conversation with Jews working the election and, specifically, an ultra-Orthodox man.

> Yemina: So he was next to me . . . and when he knew I was an Arab, he was amazed. He was like, "I always worked with Arabs, but I still feared them." . . . So, I was like, "why are you afraid of Arabs?" "Because sometimes they throw rocks on my sons, they throw rocks on me while walking by and things . . ." I was like, "don't you think the other side goes through the same thing?" He was like, "really? You know what. I really hate that." I was like, "you hate what?" He was, "I hate this Arab/Jew/Israeli kind of thing. I really want a way where we can actually live together without even experiencing or acting violent towards each other." . . . I was happy when I heard this. It was like, all these people, they're all like stereotypes. They don't like Arabs. Then you find someone from this category that people are stereotyping about that he says, "I actually don't like that." It makes me believe that it's not really black and white. You must have the white in this black category, where you must have black in this white category.

Yemina's experience at the university itself is marked by subtle discrimination (students refusing to move their backpacks to allow her to sit) and overt discrimination (a student in class avowing that the land of Israel belongs only to the Jews, an outburst that is rebuked by the professor). But, it also contains offers of help, understanding, and budding friendships with Israeli Jews and one in particular who she characterizes as a "very, very dear friend."

> A student . . . knew that I had a boyfriend. He . . . knew I was Muslim. That's how it all started. He was like, "are you Christian or Muslim?" I was like, "Muslim." He was like, "what? How (come you) don't you have the hijab on?" I was like, "it's not necessary. You don't have to put the hijab on to be a Muslim." . . . Second thing is that . . . they put Arabs in one category and then Christians in another . . . So, I also clarified that, because . . . it really pissed me off. . . . We had this kind of a connection, where I trusted him and he trusted me, and we weren't really ashamed or shy of all these questions we asked. So, he wanted to know about us and I wanted to know about him too. The way they lived, their culture, and all of these things. So, we actually talked about it. We discussed it for more than 3 to 4 hours. We sat and we just talked and talked and talked.

The above quote shows persistent misunderstandings separating the communities. However, such intimate conversations allow Yemina to communicate her experience to Israeli Jews, but also to understand their perspective. It is a meaningful exchange.

The experience at the university has also allowed Yemina to reflect on herself from a more critical perspective. When the conversation returned to her village, Yemina referenced a course reading, George Simmel's classic essay "The Stranger." She says, "I felt like he was writing about me." The essay becomes a trope for understanding various aspects of Yemina's life experience. As the only woman without a hijab, she is a stranger on the bus and treated differently from other women. Yemina and her family, liberal Muslims, are strangers in their conservative village. As a Palestinian, she is a stranger to Israeli society.

> Yemina: I really want to write something that people wouldn't know about. For instance, write about the village I live in. Or maybe how hard it was for me. It still is for me. How does it feel to feel a stranger not only in, like, the country you live in or not even in your own village, you know. Somewhere you've lived your whole life, you even feel a stranger to.
>
> Brian: So you've got a number of different strangers in your life, in a sense.
>
> Yemina: Yeah. Somehow. I mean, as Arabs, you would feel a stranger in actually a country you were born in, but under [these] circumstances, you'd have to feel that you're a stranger. You know, because it's a Jewish State. So you feel, like, you're not Jewish so you are technically a stranger. You don't have the rights as Jewish or Israeli people do, so you actually feel a stranger. . . . You know, you could go deep into it and you can find that you are a stranger . . . in various aspects. So I don't even feel as a stranger to the country. I feel a stranger with my own tribe, with my own people in my own village. So I feel it's like a strange structure of the stranger really.

Yemina's "strange structure of the stranger" nicely encapsulates the sentiment of non-belonging. She is out of place everywhere. Her critique of Palestinian social mores is sharp and biting, and she is an outsider in the Israeli social world.

But, at the end of this reflection, she offers a utopian vision, dreaming about the possibility of leaving her village for Haifa.

> Yemina: Do you want to ask me why? (Brian: Yeah, why?) First, because of the co-existence that's there. My sons, daughters . . . wouldn't feel weird or even less than the people they're living with . . . I mean, I've been to Haifa more than once and I was just free there. Like, even just

the smell of Haifa still is different. Here you feel it's like, occupation, checkpoints. You know, it's just hard living in Jerusalem and I really don't want my kids to feel that way. I want them to express themselves. I want them to have an opinion, to have a voice, to feel free, and to practice whatever they want. To be on a team with Jewish people. To be in a school with them. I don't want them to feel this Arab–Jew kind of thing.

I could end here, basking in Yemina's hopes and dreams for the future. But, this would distort the actual content of the interview. There is a significant twist that only comes at the very end of our conversation.

When closing, I ask if there is anything that she would like to add—a standard question in the interview. Yemina returns to the previous question, about historical and social events that have influenced her identity. The first time that she responded to the question, she recounted a story about a humiliating and anxiety-provoking experience at a checkpoint without her official ID card. As she says, "everything that keeps reminding me that I'm an Arab," influences my identity. "Mostly being stopped at checkpoints or being stopped by soldiers." Her second response to the question is about what happened during the Gaza war. She begins with:

So one of the attacks that happened. I mean, I wouldn't want to feel pity for it. But I would want people to know that this actually happened with me.

Yemina goes into graphic detail about a terrifying experience when masked soldiers forcibly entered her house at night, breaking the door, rousing her family from their beds, and interrogating them. The violence of the episode, recounted over several minutes, is astounding. The soldiers leave laughing when Yemina's father tells them that he is going to call the police and have the soldiers pay for the broken door. The police took the phone call, but her father fixed the door himself.

So you feel like, no matter who you are, as long as you're catego-rized as Arab, no one would give a crap about you. Like, what if my grandpa . . . had a heart attack? . . . Who would then fight against these soldiers that came and did such a thing at 3:00 a.m., you know? So you feel like no matter where you are in this society, no one would care about you if something happened to you. No one. . . . Of course, they wouldn't penetrate into Jewish houses, but even if they did, they'd be fully responsible for what happened there. Fully responsible. . . . So it makes you feel. This lack of mobility, this lack of rights, of everything.

So, yeah, these kinds of things keep reminding me. These events keep reminding me that I have to maintain this nationality in order to prove something.

I should underline the last line of this long evaluation in which Yemina says that, like the soldiers at checkpoints, these experiences work to "maintain this nationality in order to prove something."

In the interview, I am clearly struggling to make sense of the conflicting sentiments and stories that Yemina has presented. Shouldn't the violence and the humiliation of the events cause anyone to be (at the very least) spiteful? Can one dream of a future of co-existence in the face of such brutalization? Doesn't this call the rest of the interview into question? Yet, Yemina persists in holding onto her optimism in co-existence and criticizes all forms of violence. This is one of the paradoxes of her life story.

***

The end result of my analysis is rather untidy, uncovering subtleties and shades of meaning, twists and turns. This is exactly the point. Paying close attention to a single life, we find that psychological phenomena are multi-faceted, complex, dense, and, oftentimes, inconsistent. There isn't a neat and tidy statistic that we can point to. It is impossible to guess how Yemina would have answered Amara and Schnell's (2004) ratings. But, even if we did know, the simple rating of 0 to 6 wouldn't do justice to the complexity of her interpretations and reflections on identity.

In contrast, the narrative analysis captures a psychological level of human experience that is entirely absent from variable-centered analysis, bearing no resemblance to easily digestible categories and statistics. Rather, we have a sense of a full-fledged person reflecting on and interpreting their life experience and can better describe in vivid detail the dynamic process of how this person arrives at some kind of self-understanding (See Sabat, this volume). Indeed, the logic underlying Yemina's commitment, or lack thereof, to different identities is marked in the interview, in her words, and interpretable.

Yemina's identity is her own creative interpretation, but it is also contextual and, largely, relational. In my reading, Yemina's interpretations associating social relationships and identity are the connective fiber holding together her identity story. Yemina recounts that she adopted many aspects of her parents' identity, their liberal stances on matters such as women and religion and, consequently, their contested place in the extended family and the larger conservative village. These stances are reinforced by Yemina's education at an international school outside of the village and the condescending attitudes of her fellow villagers to her dress and lifestyle—most notable in her interview are interactions with her grandparents and villagers on the bus. Coming to the Hebrew University of Jerusalem presents the opportunity for intimate contact with Israeli Jews. Yemina seizes on the opportunity and engages Israeli Jews in dialogue and friendship. These experiences buttress a dream of mutual understanding and co-existence. But, the brutal realities of power relations in Israel, poignantly expressed in her encounters with Israeli soldiers, limit these aspirations and position Yemina as a second class Arab Palestinian.

Relationships are consistently referenced as decisive moments in her identity story. The end result of the push and pull of these recounted social interactions is that Yemina feels, most often, out of place and without a definite sense of her social identity. She is neither fully a part of the Arab and Palestinian world or the Israeli and Jewish one. She is a stranger to both and opts to be outside and beyond the categories effective in her social world.

Although I hope that the analysis is interesting, I believe that such rich descriptions, no matter how untidy, are of enormous scientific value. For the mainstream, such studies are considered outside the bounds of scientific psychology; at best, they are beginning points that can serve as hunches when moving to a hypothesis testing model. But, it is simply not possible to study the fundamental problems of human psychology (how persons think, feel, and interpret their actions) as statistical relationships between variables. In contrast, this is exactly the level at which a narrative analysis operates, describing how persons, in context, go about the business of making sense of their life experience.

Of course, no method is perfect and narrative analysis is no exception. Critics often point out that narrative is "merely" subjective, relying too heavily on the skills of the interpreter. Although every analysis is open to revision, the practice is anything but haphazard. It is grounded in concrete observations about what persons articulate and presented as a coherent and rational argument to a community of readers for criticism. The work is slow and painstaking, but well worth the effort. Effectively employed, qualitative methods, such as narrative analysis, provide the means for observing, as close to the action as possible, the core questions of the discipline. You just can't get there in the standard practice of variable-centered research. The only way to disclose these fundamental psychological phenomena is to study them by listening to how persons, in their own words, make interpretations connecting aspects of their life experience. For a science that prides itself on "empirical" research, the *sine qua non* of scientific research should be observations, appropriately tuned, to the phenomenon under investigation. In regards to what is most central to the discipline, narrative can do this, and variable-centered research cannot.

It is true that studying a single person does not permit the kinds of generalizations that mainstream psychologists aspire to. But, more encompassing, nuanced, theories are possible by starting with a single person and adding comparisons and refinements one by one by one.

This is the challenge that we have in front of us—to describe and understand the workings of human psychology, one person at a time, and to build a veritable psychology of meaning. In my view, this is the way that scientific psychology is done and the unique contribution that qualitative methods can make to our understanding of human psychology.

References

Amara, M., & Schnell, I. (2004). Identity repertoires among Arabs in Israel. *Journal of Ethnic Migration Studies, 30*(1), 175–193.

Central Bureau of Statistics State of Israel. (2008). *The Arab population in Israel.* Retrieved July 27, 2017 from www.cbs.gov.il/www/statistical/arab_pop08e.pdf.

Central Bureau of Statistics State of Israel. (2008/2009). *Students at universities, by degree, sex, age, population group, religion and place of birth* (Table 2.14). Retrieved July 27, 2017 from www.cbs.gov.il/publications12/1475_haskhala_gvoha08_09/pdf/t2_14.pdf.

Danziger, K. (1997). *Naming the mind: How psychology found its language.* Thousand Oaks, CA: Sage Publications.

Hoffman, J. E., & Rouhana, N. (1976). Young Arabs in Israel: Some aspects of a conflicted social identity. *The Journal of Social Psychology, 99,* 75–86.

Lamiell, J. T. (2003). *Beyond individual and group differences: Human individuality, scientific psychology, and William Stern's critical personalism.* Thousand Oaks, CA: Sage Publications.

Pappé, I. (2011). *The forgotten Palestinians: A history of the Palestinians in Israel.* New Haven, CT: Yale University Press.

Peres, Y., & Yuval-Davis, N. (1969). Some observations on the national identity of the Israeli Arab. *Human Relations, 22*(3), 219–233.

Rabinowitz, D., & Abu-Baker, K. (2005). *Coffins on our shoulders: The experience of Palestinian citizens of Israel.* Berkeley, CA: The University of California Press.

Rouhana, N. (1997). *Palestinian citizens in an ethnic Jewish state: Identities in conflict.* New Haven, CT: Yale University Press.

Schiff, B. (2002). Talking about identity: Arab students at the Hebrew University of Jerusalem. *Ethos, 30*(3), 273–303.

Schiff, B. (2017). *A new narrative for psychology.* New York, NY: Oxford University Press.

Smooha, S. (1999). The advances and limits of the Israelization of Israel's Palestinian citizens. In K. Abdel-Malek & D. C. Jacobson (Eds.), *Israeli and Palestinian identities in history and literature* (pp. 9–33). New York, NY: St. Martin's Press.

Smooha, S. (2005). *Index of Arab- Jewish relations in Israel 2004.* Haifa: The Jewish- Arab Center, University of Haifa.

7 Qualitative Psychology's Coming of Age

Are There Grounds for Hope?

Mark Freeman

As Brian Schiff suggests in the introductory chapter to this volume, qualitative psychology has come of age—or is at least in the process of doing so. The Society for Qualitative Inquiry in Psychology has found (something of) a home within Division 5 of the American Psychological Association, *Qualitative Psychology* is a well-respected journal in the field (at least by those who respect it), an article on reporting standards for qualitative research was recently published in the *American Psychologist*, and more. So it is that some of us now speak of the *promises* of qualitative inquiry (Gergen, Josselson, & Freeman, 2015), seeing in the qualitative movement a vitally important inroad into meaningfully transforming the discipline. Indeed, I myself penned an article not too long ago with the rather audacious title, "Qualitative Inquiry and the Self-Realization of Psychological Science" (Freeman, 2014), my argument essentially being that, now that qualitative inquiry had begun to enter the scene of psychology "proper," we might finally be in the process of crafting a true science—which is to say, one more adequate to the human condition than the reductive, objectifying one that had held sway throughout most of the discipline's history. The developments just referred to are positive ones, indeed. The promises of qualitative inquiry are many. And yes, I continue to believe that, slowly but surely, the discipline is maturing, "realizing" itself, by at least casting into question some of its defensive, narcissistic methodolatry, and opening itself to new ways of being, ones more conducive to reciprocity and mutual respect.

All of this, it would seem, is *hopeful*. Why, then, ask the question that stands as the title of this concluding chapter? I do succumb to moments of cynicism, still. There remain aspects of the discipline that continue to strike me as nothing short of scandalous. And for all the progress that's being made, it remains difficult, for me at any rate, to avoid seeing psychology as an immense, largely immoveable, monolith, that is so wrongheaded in much of what it does that it would require nothing short of a collective brain transplant to truly right its ways. There. I've had my rant. Can I return to hope now? Sure. But of what sort?

Reconciliation or Revolution?

For Schiff, "The overarching problem of this volume" concerns "situating qualitative methods in scientific psychology." Bearing this problem in mind, he goes on to raise three substantive questions: "(1) What has been, is, and should be, the relationship between quantitative and qualitative methods? (2) Are qualitative methods a part of psychological science or are they something else? and (3) What is the unique contribution of qualitative methods in the production of psychological knowledge?" (p. 3). About the first of these questions, Schiff (in concert with Wertz, among others) suggests that, Manichean appearances notwithstanding, quantitative and qualitative methods need not be seen as "mutually exclusive" or agonistic. Indeed, following Slaney and Tafreshi in broad outline, he states, "At the heart of the emerging methodological inclusiveness is the argument that qualitative and quantitative methods can be fruitfully, and pragmatically, integrated according to the nature of the research question under investigation" (p. 4). This, in essence, is the reconciliation argument, and there is much to recommend it. There is not much ground to be gained by methodological polarization, and, by all indications, there is a good deal of ground to be gained through the kind of integration being proposed. "Rather than perpetuate the myth that qualitative and quantitative methods are mutually exclusive and incompatible," therefore,

> the discipline should embrace possibilities for new models of the research enterprise. In a sense, methods, quantitative and qualitative, can be viewed as value-neutral tools that, skillfully and meticulously applied, can provide evidence to help us think through particular research questions.
>
> (p. 5)

I confess: I just felt a twinge of cynicism return. Value-neutral tools? I don't know about this. And if truth be told, I am increasingly unsure about the reconciliation project more generally.

But let me set my uncertainty aside for now and move on to Schiff's second question, concerning whether qualitative methods are to be considered part of psychological science. As Schiff rightly notes, "The problem of method . . . is closely related to fundamental conceptions of what constitutes science." He is also right to note that, "Typically, psychologists consider quantitative methods as *the* one and only 'scientific' psychology and place qualitative methods in some other marginal category—perhaps art, literature, journalism, or philosophy but not psychological science." Are these characterizations warranted? "Are qualitative methods any less scientific than quantitative ones? Do qualitative methods fundamentally change the meaning of psychological science?" (p. 5) For good and compelling reasons, Schiff is reluctant to have quantitative methods corner the market on psychological science; thinking in this way is parochial and exclusionary. Can't qualitative methods be considered scientific too? They can, Schiff answers, but only if we adopt a more capacious and inclusive conception of science than the one typically employed in academic psychology.

As Schiff goes on to acknowledge, some qualitative psychologists view their work "as outside of the narrow frame of science." Most, however, "understand their research as employing *a* scientific method and reject the characterization of their research as somehow standing outside of scientific psychology" (p. 6). In this context too, therefore, Schiff's perspective, and the perspective of the volume as a whole, aims toward reconciliation. There will no doubt have to be some fancy conceptual inversions along the way. Citing my own (2011) work on "poetic science," for instance, he notes that "the pathway to a fruitful scientific psychology might entail the inclusion of methods, deceptively artistic or literary in their style, which are better suited to describing certain aspects of human psychology" (p. 7). *Deceptively* artistic or literary? I don't know about this either. And if truth be told once again, I am increasingly unsure about the desire—including, for the most part, my own—to continue to march under the banner of "science." Why do so, anyway? There are unquestionably political reasons for doing so. If we want to be part of the club, we need to play by the rules of the game— bending them when we can, of course, to suit our own interests. There are also historical reasons for doing so. Whether we like it or not, psychology sought to become a science, that's what it pretty much became, so we need to work as best as we can within the current idiom. That's what *disciplines* do. At times, however, I have come to feel that ideas such as poetic science are somehow disingenuous, that they entail shoehorning things into a shoe that really may not fit (Freeman, 2015).

But let me set aside my uncertainty once more. Turning to Schiff's third question, regarding the unique contribution of qualitative methods in the production of psychological knowledge, we are reminded that "some psychological phenomena are difficult or even impossible to quantify" and that "when we start to explore the realm of human experience and meaning making," we find that "quantitative methods are clumsy and, oftentimes, misleading tools." Nevertheless, they are still employed. "No justifications are required; it is just assumed that all psychological phenomena can be studied with quantitative tools." In this third context, the issues seem to be heating up. "This is a dangerous assumption," Schiff goes on to say, and, as Lamiell, especially, has argued, it "leads to numerous errors in our understanding of the dynamics of human psychology" (p. 8). Particularly problematic, for Lamiell, is when psychologists believe that using group-level statistical analyses can help them understand individual persons. Doing so is nothing less than a "fatal, logical error," and it has resulted in much of psychology essentially being a version of demography.

Is there room for reconciliation here? Perhaps; it may be argued that, by bringing qualitative inquiry into the methodological picture, we have in hand a much-needed idiographic complement to the reigning view and that between the two perspectives—for simplicity's sake, the nomothetic and the idiographic—we can have a much more comprehensive and adequate psychology. "By making visible the ways that persons construct and connect their experiences, how they reason and think through self and world," Schiff writes, "qualitative methods are a corrective force" (p. 12) to the group-level perspective Lamiell and others have criticized. They are also a corrective to the largely decontextualized view of knowledge promulgated in much of psychology. "Psychological phenomena are not static variables but are part of the thoughts and lives of real persons, who are engaged in social relationships, and embedded in history and culture," and qualitative methods are uniquely suited to precisely these "real-life" phenomena, able to provide the needed language "for more dense and complex descriptions of *how*, *where*, and *when* persons think, feel, or act in order to develop synthetic theories about *why*" (p. 9).

As Schiff acknowledges, the discipline could elect to bar these phenomena from view, and push their study to other disciplines. It "could draw a sharp line and say that psychology is not concerned with how persons, alone and together, make sense of themselves and the world and relegate these core psychological problems to other disciplines." This is essentially what it *has* done. It is time, therefore, to "enlarge the scope of inquiry and welcome innovative methods of studying and theorizing about psychology into the center of the conversation," and the only way to foster this progress is "when a productive relationship between qualitative and quantitative methods develops" (p. 9).

On most days, I would agree with just about everything Schiff and the others in this volume have to say about the virtues of reconciliation. As Lamiell suggests in his chapter, there do appear to grounds for hope for at least "softening," if not eliminating, "the abiding resistance" (p. 11) to qualitative methods. For Lamiell, perhaps more than any of the others, the process is a daunting one, not only because of the dominance of quantitative methods, but also because of the continuing (mis)use of population-level statistical methods as a means of understanding individual-level phenomena. As the saying goes, old habits die hard; and this particular one is so thoroughly, and perniciously, ingrained into the pantheon of contemporary academic psychology that disabusing people of it is bound to remain an uphill battle. (He has been trying, mightily, for a long time.) The good news is that qualitative psychology does indeed seem to be coming of age and would appear to be pointing the way toward the more capacious view of science that Schiff had called for.

Slaney and Tafreshi appear to be less burdened by the kinds of problems Lamiell identified in his chapter and thus more hopeful about psychology getting its act together. For them, what's most needed at this juncture is a "pluralistic, tool-based methodology, within which research questions and aims serve a key role in informing and guiding methods choices" (p. 27). Regarding the idea that quantitative and qualitative methods are philosophically incompatible—sensibly referred to as the "incompatibility thesis"—they suggest that the thesis "rests on weak footings, . . . that there is a possibility of meaningful interplay between quantitative and qualitative research traditions within the field of psychology," and that "wedding" the two "does not necessarily lead to epistemological incoherence" (p. 35). Having attended several "weddings" of quantitative and qualitative psychology in recent years, I feel obliged to note that, generally, they have been extremely awkward and uncomfortable. (There is no question but that some people on both sides of the Division 5 "marriage" have entertained divorce and possibly even annulment, the latter owing to the idea that this particular betrothal is downright *illegitimate*.) But this appears to be more of a cultural matter than an epistemological one. Give it time, some have said. There are bound to be tensions. Let's see if we can make this work. The key is to adopt an abiding "methodological pluralism, . . . informed by a critically pragmatic philosophical orientation." This "may provide an impetus for psychology to examine its methodological assumptions and thereby promote a deeper understanding of problems with the methods that have been privileged and, hopefully, greater freedom to develop new and innovative methods" (p. 39).

We see such hope continuing apace in Wertz's chapter as well. The fact is, "Psychology's identification of science with quantitative methods and failure to recognize the fundamental importance of qualitative methods has left a major gap at the heart of the science itself" (p. 46). For Wertz, we are finally in the process of filling that gap, and as long as we remain committed to the sort of rigor science requires, we will be one step closer to building the inclusive, pluralistic science many desire. Not unlike Slaney and Tafreshi, Wertz is eager to move beyond the incompatibility thesis: "It can no longer be assumed that philosophies of science and theoretical traditions are incommensurable." What's more, "mixed methods research," in particular, "fruitfully demonstrates compatibility" (p. 52). Indeed, "Contemporary integrations of qualitative and quantitative methods are teaching us that, even as distinctive as each may be, these two ways of knowing can be overlapping and inseparable" (p. 53).

Gergen's perspective, although aligned in some ways with both Slaney and Tafresi and Wertz, moves in a somewhat different direction. "The qualitative movement in psychology," he writes, "now harbors the potential to radically transform the contours of the discipline," and "the effects of this transformation would vastly expand the contribution of the discipline to society—and to the world" (p. 61). Gergen's brand of hope is for more than a nice, if somewhat awkward, wedding. "There is a heady sense that a new door has opened, and new horizons of inquiry are there to be explored" (p. 64). Some of these will be in the service of building the kind of science many desire. But others may have entirely different aims and purposes. For Gergen, "There are no overarching ontological agreements, epistemological assumptions, set of values, or conception of research goals that unite the various endeavors now constituting the qualitative movement in psychology." Instead, we encounter "multiplicities," "hybrids," and "new creations." All of these are part of "the qualitative explosion," and all signal the idea that "there is a marked absence of attempts to elevate any given orientation over the other, or to undermine or disqualify the alternatives" (p. 68).

Gergen's pluralism is more than a methodological pluralism, and while he is certainly interested in expanding the purview of psychological science, he also seems to suggest that we need not be bound by this goal. Indeed, more important, on some level, than the goal of expanding the space of scientificity is expanding the space of *action*: "As our frames of understanding increase, so do we locate new possibilities for action—for support, intervention, social change, policy formation and so on." Along these lines, "the qualitative movement brings with it a re-invigoration of values. . . . Ushered into presence by the movement is an invaluable sensitivity to the ethical/ideological dimensions of research", which in turn allows reflection on research to move "beyond the traditional confinement to methods and results to the ethical and political consequences" (pp. 69–70). In this context too, therefore, "There are many reasons to hope that the new pluralism signifies a major transformation of the discipline" (p. 71). Gergen would appear to be more oriented toward revolution than reconciliation. It is, however, a gentle one, geared in the end toward a kind of multi-perspectival, multi-cultural, multi-purpose festival. All are welcome. All belong.

With Sabat's chapter and Schiff's penultimate chapter, we move into some qualitative particulars and, in doing so, are able to gain a still clearer, more concrete sense of the value of qualitative inquiry. Sabat's inquiry into Alzheimer's disease (AD), which draws upon Luria's "Romantic Science" approach to neuropsychological matters, is seen as "complementary" to the more standard quantitative approaches that tend to be employed. The key is to focus precisely on *persons* with AD—to see them as "semiotic subject[s] rather than as someone whose condition can be understood fully in quantitative terms by his or her scores on standard tests" (p. 75). As Sabat writes, "There are no standard neuropsychological tests or other medical means of evaluating people with AD that would have revealed or predicted the semiotic behavior exemplified in these people's actions" (p. 79). By taking a qualitative approach, on the other hand, significant gains can be made.

Schiff offers a similar point of view in his story of Yemina. Like Sabat, he acknowledges that "psychology's method of choice is not equipped to observe how psychological phenomena play out in thoughts, experiences, and reflections of persons" (p. 85). On the contrary: "Rather than dealing with the workings of psychological phenomena, researchers are left with decontextualized and disembodied fragments without a good sense of how psychological relationships function in the experience of persons" (p. 86). For that, once again, we need to look at *persons*—in this case, *narratives* of persons; only then will we truly be able to speak to the realities of experience. Yemina's story—or Schiff's rendition of Yemina's story—is interesting, revealing, and, at times, moving. It also ends in a wonderfully open-ended way, and is as much about questions as it is answers. Indeed, Schiff avows, "The end result of my analysis is rather untidy, uncovering subtleties and shades of meaning, twists and turns. This is exactly the point," he adds. "Paying close attention to a single life, we find that psychological phenomena are multifaceted, complex, dense, and, oftentimes, inconsistent" (p. 97). All true, unquestionably. And "such rich descriptions, no matter how untidy, are of enormous scientific value" (p. 98). The reason: "For a science that prides itself on 'empirical' research, the *sine qua non* of scientific research should be observations, appropriately tuned, to the phenomenon under investigation." And the fact of the matter is, "narrative can do this and variable-centered research cannot" (p. 98).

It seems almost churlish to quibble with any of this. In fact, I have made much the same argument myself and have suggested that qualitative work can lead us beyond the *faux* empiricism found in much of the discipline, toward true empiricism—that is, one that, above all, seeks and practices fidelity to the phenomena. But as I have confessed already, I have begun to wonder about this stance. Has Schiff been doing science when telling and analyzing Yemina's story? Have I been doing it when I write about my mother's dementia? On one level, the answer to these questions is immaterial. It is what it is; call it whatever you want. Seen this way, I have no qualms whatsoever about Schiff calling what he's doing science. Who am I to say? What, then, is the problem? More to the point, why might it be important—in some instances—to move beyond the discourse of science when thinking about qualitative work? My goal, in raising these questions, is not to dash the hopes of those who have written for this volume! Indeed, I too believe there are grounds for hope. But it may be a bit different than what we have seen throughout most of these pages.

What Are the Grounds of Hope?

It is only fitting that I begin this last section with a few qualifications. First, lest one assume that what I am about to say bespeaks some sort of anti-quantification sentiment, let me hasten to emphasize that indicting quantitative work as a whole would be silly and wrong; there are dimensions of psychological inquiry for which quantitative methods are wonderfully well-suited. I also believe that mixed methods approaches can be useful, that there are ways in which quantitative and qualitative work bleed into one another, and that setting up the relationship between the two as some sort of fierce battle owing to their ultimate irreconcilability is utterly pointless. Finally, I, like all of the others in this volume, am excited and hopeful about the possibility of qualitative inquiry contributing to a more inclusive, capacious, and pluralistic view of science than the one currently in place. But since I was asked to write this concluding chapter and happen to actually *have* some of the uncertainties that have been voiced, I thought it might be useful to take this chapter in a somewhat different direction. I therefore ask again: What's the problem?

I can think of at least two responses to this question. The first, about which I will be mercifully brief, concerns the default assumption that psychology is and must be a science. It didn't have to be. And it doesn't have to be. We in qualitative circles have gotten adept at proclaiming and arguing that it doesn't have to be *that* kind of science: reductive, scientistic, and misconceived; *die Geisteswissenschaften* were a kind of science too. But we still hold onto the idea that it ought to be a science of some sort. Here, I fear that my response will sound just a tad juvenile. *Who says?!* Again, I realize that there are all kinds of reasons why it makes sense to stay the scientific course (broadly conceived), including, especially, political ones. But I seem to have finally reached a point at which my own would-be remaking of what science is and does has come to seem not only disingenuous but unnecessary. I don't think this means that the idea of science has to be given over to "them"—that is, those who have assumed they owned the idea. There certainly remains substantial room for remaking it, in just the way many of us have tried to do. But the science game isn't the only one in town, and to assume that it is, I suggest, is to acquiesce to a stance that neither is nor ought to be the last word. With this in mind, I would only ask that we at least consider what else qualitative psychology might be *besides* science.

Let me, however, turn to a more substantive reason for raising this issue by saying a few words about a symposium I participated in several years ago at the Narrative Matters conference in Paris. The question for the symposium was: "Do narratives sum?" That is, could we somehow pool the "findings" derived from the various stories we gather and build an edifice of scientific knowledge? My initial response was that this question can't be answered definitively one way or the other. And the reason—or a reason—is that it all depends on what kind of narrative work is being done. On one end of the continuum of narrative inquiry, there is work that simply "uses" narratives (so to speak) as a way of talking about something else: adolescent identity formation, the process of aging, whatever. Insofar as the primary focus of exploring narratives is essentially *informational*—that is, geared toward specific informant populations (e.g., contemporary adolescents) or content areas (e.g., identity formation)—the goal is an important one: The knowledge at hand is essentially "detachable" from the specific narratives from which they derive. So it is that we can, and do, learn something about "adolescence" or "aging" from such narratives. Even here, in this most explicitly scientific context, the accumulated knowledge may be ephemeral because narratives are works of culture and history that change across place and time. There is also the retrospective and reconstructive dimension of narratives, and this too may be seen as working against the aim of summation. But there is no reason, I think, to question the summative aspect of narratives in cases like the ones just referred to.

On the other end of the continuum of narrative inquiry are more "fully storied" approaches, which seek to let the narrative or narratives in question (and I say this cautiously) "speak for themselves." In this context, I shall take the liberty of referring briefly to more recent work I have done concerning my mother, who died 2 years ago at age 93 after having spent approximately a decade with dementia. In this form of narrative knowing, there is no detaching the content of what is said from the form of its presentation. In this respect, I would suggest, there is an irreducible particularity to language itself that renders narrative knowing, and certain forms of qualitative knowing more generally, different in kind and order from the sort of knowing that the project of accumulation generally relies upon.

Here, then, I am speaking about the fact that the medium—in this case, language—is not to be seen as a mere vehicle, or means, for transmitting this or that bit of information but is significant in its own right: sensuously, tonally, musically. In this mode of narrative work, in other words, the medium *matters* in a different way than it does in more standard forms of social science research. Referring to Jay Parini (from his book *Why Poetry Matters*), "Words are symbols, and—as such—have resonance beyond their literal meanings. They gesture in directions that cannot be pinned down, and strike chords in the unconscious mind" (2008, p. 179). For Parini, there may even be a spiritual dimension to the process. In my view, then, this idea of drawing on the sensuous qualities of the medium—in this case, using language in such a way that it not only "conveys" but expresses and evokes, even *moves*—is an important one, and one that would appear to militate against the summative project. Generally, we read narrative work, and qualitative work more generally, to become informed, to understand, this or that phenomenon. But we can also read such research for its meaning and possible beauty. This sort of work resists pure conceptualization, carrying forth a kind of poetic resonance that exceeds concept, grasp, understanding (see Gadamer, 1986).

What exactly is the value of this more literary, art-ful form of narrative inquiry we have just been considering? Among other things, it further humanizes us, and serves to enlarge our sense of who and what we are. It can also serve to awaken us to what is *other*, and strengthen our powers of empathy, sympathy, and compassion. If I am writing about my mother, I certainly want to contribute to knowledge in some way: about dementia, or memory, or identity, or being a son. I have to be cautious in how I do so, of course; she is just one "case," after all. I also want to write about her in a way that might be moving at times, in just the way literature can be. Most important, though, I want readers to see her, and feel her, in her particularity, her otherness—another human being, living, suffering, loving. Along these lines, one index of significance in narrative work of this sort has to do with the degree to which readers are brought to encounter and appreciate the difference and otherness of others, whoever they may be, and, at the same time, brought to see their humanness and proximity, their existence as fellow travelers, brothers and sisters, fathers and mothers.

In keeping with the aforementioned idea of "poetic science," I would reiterate here that there can be a kind of deep scientificity found in narrative work—by which I mean a level of adequacy, and fidelity, to the phenomena in question, the (proverbial) "things themselves." One might even speak of "objectivity" in this context—not the kind that comes from observational detachment, precise measures, and so on, but an objectivity that, in a sense, *precedes* such measures, that seeks to be faithful to its object, however ambiguous, multiple, and messy it may be. Great literature does this wonderfully well; it gives us a possible world, one that somehow articulates reality, gives it flesh and form. In this respect, paradoxically, great literature is never far from the kind of deep scientificity and objectivity I have been considering. And neither is quality narrative work. In it, there is often what might be called a kind of resonant particularity, a mode of narrative expression that, even in its particularity, moves beyond itself and thus bears within it a measure of generality or universality.

Do narratives sum? Sometimes. Do I care whether the work I do is considered science? Sometimes. But other times I really don't. Some might protest at this point and want to ask, "Well, then, what distinguishes what you do from storytellers, poets, and other such full-fledged humanists?" This is an intellectual division-of-labor issue, and they are right to ask it. But my answer would be: at times, nothing at all—except, perhaps, the context in which we put our work forward. Put a given piece of well-crafted narrative in a literary magazine, and it's "art." Put it in an academic journal, where there might be a more explicit empirical or theoretical context within which the piece can be located, and it's "science." So, while some narratives do indeed sum, others don't; and by speaking for themselves, they can be extremely valuable in their own right.

In closing, however, I want to offer one additional qualification, and it has to do with the very idea of general knowledge, of the sort that is implicated in the idea and ideal of narratives summing. Here, I am thinking again about the idea that there is a kind of generalizing, or even universalizing, dimension that is essentially built-in to the work of art. What this in turn implies is that even in those instances of narrative work where nothing at all is being explicitly done to draw out the relevant conclusions—that is, where there is just narrative, resonant, and beautiful, speaking to our spirit and heart—there can remain, immanent within the text, a dimension of meaning that transcends its own particularity. Put another way, there can remain a dimension of meaning that, within this very particularity, transcends itself. In this context, we might ask: What is the significance of the fact that literature, and art more generally, is often able to speak to the complexities of human lives with an urgency, an intensity, and an evocative power scarcely found in psychology? And what are the implications of these facts for re-imagining and reconstructing the discipline?

I have come to think that the answers to these questions are quite clear. Literature, in particular, "lends itself" to capturing and expressing the complexities of human lives in a way that science generally does not. Can qualitative psychologists speak to these complexities with a comparable level of urgency, intensity, and evocative power to that found in literature? I certainly don't see why not. What this in turn suggests is that, alongside the good and worthy project of expanding the purview of psychological science through qualitative inquiry is the project of imagining and constructing entirely new ways of conceiving the discipline. These new ways are squarely rooted in the arts and humanities. By clearing an adequate space for them, psychology may finally succeed in becoming more adequate to the human condition and thereby further realize itself as a discipline.

Coda: Qualitative Inquiry and the Future of Psychology

There are two ways to understand the phrase "Qualitative Psychology's Coming of Age." Seen from one angle, the idea would be that qualitative psychology *has* come of age. Seen from another angle, the phrase could be taken to mean that qualitative psychology is *in the process* of coming of age. (It all hinges on the meaning of the apostrophe.) From the first angle, in other words, the argument could be made that we do, finally, have our proverbial foot in the door, that we have arrived, that we're part of the scientific enterprise, now expanded. From the second, the argument could be made that we are still emerging and evolving and that in addition to the goal of being part of this worthy enterprise, there is, as above, the goal of re-imagining, radically, what else the discipline of psychology might be. In keeping with this second rendition, I guess one could say that it is time to adopt what in Buddhist circles is sometimes called "beginner's mind." This entails casting aside, to the greatest extent possible, extant categories and preconceptions, and encountering anew what is there to see. This will likely eventuate not only in "science" and "art," but also, perhaps, work that will dismantle and dissolve these very categories as well as the boundaries customarily thought to exist between them. So, yes, absolutely: There are grounds for hope, and they go deep. Some of this hope is found in the pages of this volume. And some will be found in the future, as qualitative psychology continues to thrive, create, and grow.

References

Freeman, M. (2011). Toward poetic science. *Integrative Psychological and Behavioral Science, 45*, 389–396. doi:10.1007/s12124-011-9171-x

Freeman, M. (2014). Qualitative inquiry and the self-realization of psychological science. *Qualitative Inquiry, 20*, 119–126.

Freeman, M. (2015). Narrative psychology as science and as art. In J. Valsiner, G. Marsico, N. Chaudhary, T. Sato, & V. Dazzani (Eds.), *Psychology as a science of human being: The yokohama manifesto* (pp. 349–364). Cham, Switzerland: Springer.

Gadamer, H.-G. (1986). *The relevance of the beautiful and other essays*. Cambridge: Cambridge University Press.

Gergen, K. J., Josselson, R., & Freeman, M. (2015). The promises of qualitative inquiry. *American Psychologist, 70*, 1–9.

Parini, J. (2008). *Why poetry matters*. New Haven, CT: Yale University Press.

Index

Printed in the United States
by Baker & Taylor Publisher Services